Caroline Hazard

The Narragansett Friends' Meeting in the XVIII Century

Caroline Hazard

The Narragansett Friends' Meeting in the XVIII Century

ISBN/EAN: 9783337405274

Printed in Europe, USA, Canada, Australia, Japan

Cover: Foto ©Lupo / pixelio.de

More available books at www.hansebooks.com

THE
Narragansett Friends' Meeting

IN THE XVIII CENTURY

WITH A CHAPTER ON QUAKER BEGINNINGS
IN RHODE ISLAND

BY

CAROLINE HAZARD

BOSTON AND NEW YORK
HOUGHTON, MIFFLIN AND COMPANY
The Riverside Press, Cambridge
1899

PREFACE

THIS little book has grown from a paper read before the Rhode Island Historical Society in September, 1894. In presenting it I mentioned the name of my master, the late Professor Diman, to whose inspiring teaching and example I owe an increasing debt of gratitude. And so I want to write his name here, knowing that his training is an abiding force in the lives of his pupils.

C. H.

OAKWOODS IN PEACE DALE, R. I.
September 25, 1899.

CONTENTS

Page

CHAPTER I. QUAKER BEGINNINGS IN RHODE
ISLAND 3
Correspondence with Massachusetts. The arrival of the *Woodhouse* at Newport. Quakers driven from Massachusetts. Cruel laws. Mary Dyer and her companions. Her sentence and reprieve. Her death.

CHAPTER II. THE ESTABLISHMENT OF THE
SOUTH KINGSTOWN MONTHLY MEETING . . . 41
Disturbed conditions in Rhode Island. Visit of George Fox. The Greenwich meeting. The meeting divided.

CHAPTER III. THE MEETING-HOUSES . . . 59
The records. The "Old Meeting-house." The Clerk and Treasurer. Westerly Meetinghouses. Matunuck Meeting-house. Richmond Meeting-house. Repairs and accounts. Youths' meetings.

CHAPTER IV. THE CLERKS OF THE MEETING 77
Peter Davis. Stephen Hoxsie. Peleg Peckham. Thomas Hazard. The Overseers and Queries.

CHAPTER V. THE WORK OF THE MEETING . 95
Surrounding churches. Friends' discipline. New Lights. Temperance. Fighting. Suing at law. Debtors. Traveling.

CHAPTER VI. THE WOMEN'S MEETING . . . 117
  Clerks of the Women's meeting. Preaching Friends. Patience Greene. Marriages with dancing and vain mirth. Marriage in shifts.

CHAPTER VII. SLAVERY 139
  John Woolman. Testimony of Richard Smith in 1757. The Rathbun case. Slavery in the Women's meeting.

CHAPTER VIII. THE REVOLUTION 159
  Jeffrey Watson's diary. Nailor Tom's diary. Sufferings by war. Good government. Results of the meeting.

I
QUAKER BEGINNINGS IN RHODE ISLAND

I

Aquidneck's isle, Nantucket's lonely shores,
  And Indian-haunted Narragansett saw
The way-worn travellers round their camp-fire draw,
Or heard the plashing of their weary oars.
And every place whereon they rested grew
  Happier for pure and gracious womanhood,
  And men whose names for stainless honor stood,
Founders of states and rulers wise and true.
                                WHITTIER.

THE first mention of Quakers in the records of the Colony of Rhode Island occurs in the year 1657, when a letter arrived from the commissioners of the United Colonies addressed to the governor of Rhode Island:

The commiffioners being informed that divers Quakers are arrived this summer at Rode Ifland and entertained there, which may prove dangerous to the Collonies, thought meet to manifeft theire minds to the Governor there as followeth : —

GENT: — We suppofe you have underftood that the laft yeare a companie of Quakers arived at Bofton vpon noe other account than to difperfe theire pernicious opinions had they not been prevented by the prudent care of that Government, . . . whoe vpon that occafion commended it to the General Courts of the United Collonies that all Quakers Ranters & such notorious heretiques might be prohibited coming amongſt vs.[1]

The "prudent care" of the authorities of Boston and the Bay towns is well known. Fines, imprisonment, and whipping at the cart's tail all fell within the limits of prudence; and, not content with care for their own colony, the letter goes on to say:

We thinke noe care too great to preferve us from such a peft, the contagion whereof (if received) within youer Collonie were dangerous, &c, to be defused to the other by means of the intercourfe especially to the place of trade amongſt us — Wee therefore make it our requeſt that you, as well as the reſt of the Collonies take such order herein that youre naighbours may be freed from that danger; that you remove thofe Quakers that have been receaved, and for the future prohibite theire cominge amongſt you.[2]

[1] R. I. C. R., vol. i. p. 374.
[2] R. I. C. R., vol. i. p. 374-375.

This letter is dated Boston, September 12, 1657, and signed "Simon Bradstreet, president." Mr. Bartlett, the learned compiler of the Rhode Island Colonial Records, points out that while the commissioners demanded the expulsion of Quakers from Rhode Island, the Massachusetts government were sending Quakers into the colony, as in the case of Humphrey Norton.

The Quakers who caused this concern of mind to the honorable commissioners had come to Aquidneck from England, and had been kindly received. Indeed, they could hardly have found a place in the world of that day where more people, by inheritance and tradition, would have been inclined to welcome them. The town of Newport was not yet twenty years old, being an offshoot from the first settlement on the island at Portsmouth. It was Portsmouth which gave Mrs. Hutchinson an asylum when her teaching had become too mystical for the rigid theology of Boston. "With her," says Professor Diman, "religion was less a creed than an inner experience; to her enthusiastic faith, the Holy Ghost seemed actually to unite itself with the soul of the justified person."[1] Nicholas Easton, who built the

[1] Sir Henry Vane, J. L. Diman, *Orations and Essays*.

first house at Newport, seems to have shared her beliefs, though doubtless with differences, for Rhode Island soon became famous for its divergence of opinion. According to Winthrop, he was "a man very bold, though ignorant," and much exercised on the question of man's will and God's sovereignty. He maintained "that man has no power or will of himſelf, but as he is acted upon by God. Being shown what blasphemous conſequence would follow hereνpon, they profeſſed to abhor the conſequences, but ſtill defended the propoſitions which," Winthrop adds, "diſcovered their ignorance."[1] Samuel Gorton, also a mystic, had been found even too mystical for the company on the island, and, after a short and troublous sojourn at Portsmouth, betook himself and his doctrines across the Bay, where he founded Warwick. So the spiritual atmosphere of the island was prepared for the arrival of Friends in 1657 far more than any of the other settlements could have been.

The reply of the colony of Rhode Island to the letter of the commissioners shows the curious mixture of liberality and prejudice

[1] Arnold's *History of Rhode Island*, p. 152.

characteristic of the founders. Benedict Arnold was president of the colony, and he, with William Baulston, Randall Houlden, as he writes his name, Arthur Fenner and William Field, sign the very interesting letter which was sent in reply, dated October 13, 1657: —

Our defires are, they declare, in all things poffible, to purfue after and keep fayre and loveinge correfpondence and entercourfe with all the collonys, and with all our countrymen in New England, . . . by giving juftice to any that demand it among us, and by returning fuch as make efcape from you, or from other colonys, being fuch as fly from the hands of juftice for matters of crime done or committed amongft you, &c. And as concerning thefe quakers (so called) which are now amongft us, we have no law among us whereby to punifh any for only declaring by words, &c, theire mindes and underftandings concerning the things and ways of God as to falvation and an eternal condition.

Here we have a distinct declaration of the limits of the civil power, a declaration as far in advance of the times as Roger

Williams himself, and breathing his spirit, if not actually inspired by him. And yet, immediately following this noble sentence, the letter continues in the spirit of its own day : —

And, moreover, we find that in thofe places where thefe people aforefaid in this coloney are moft of all suffered to declare themfelves freely, and are only oppofed by arguments in difcourfe, there they leaft of all defire to come, and we are informed that they begin to loath this place, for that they are not oppofed by the civill authority, but with all patience and meek- nefs are suffered to fay over their pre- tended revelations and admonitions, nor are they like or able to gain many more to their way . . . and yet we conceive that their doctrines tend to very abfolute cutting downe and overturninge religious and civill government among men if gen- erally received.

This letter was addressed " to the much honoured the General Court sitting at Bos- ton for the Collony of Maffachusetts."[1] Thus, while agreeing with the Massachu- setts authorities as to the evil influence of

[1] R. I. C. R., vol. i. p. 378.

the Quakers, the Rhode Island men held fast to their principle of religious liberty. Six months later the question was taken up by the general assembly sitting at Portsmouth, and a letter was sent " To the much honored John Endicott, Governor of the Massachusetts," which is even more explicit. Quakers, this letter declares, " are generally conceived pernicious, either intentionally, or at least wise in efect, even to the corruptinge of good manners and difturbinge the common peace and focieties of the places where they arife or refort unto," etc.

" Now, whereas freedom of different confciences, to be protected from inforcements was the principle ground of our Charter both with respect to our humble fute for it, as alfo to the true intent of the Honorable and renowned parleiment of England in grantinge of the same to us ; which freedom we still prize as the greateft hapiness that men can pofefs in this world:

" Therefore we shall for the prefervation of our civill peace and order the more ferioufly take notice," the letter continues, to have Quakers conform in all civil things, " as traynings, watchings and such other ingadgements," and will inquire from England as to a proper course to pursue, being informed that many Quakers are "suffered to live in England, yea, even in the heart of the nation." John Sandford, clerk of the assembly, signs this letter, but here again the spirit, if not the hand, of Roger Williams is evident. No one could prize more than he the "freedom of different confciences," and no one was more ready to extend this "greateft hapiness that men can pofefs in this world" to others.

The Quakers who were the subjects of these letters from Massachusetts arrived at Newport in the little ship Woodhouse, Robert Fowler master, during the summer of 1657.[1] He was a North of England man, and, while building his ship, became convinced, and had a divine intimation, that the ship he was then building should be devoted to the use of the society he had joined. In July of the previous year, (1656), Mary Fisher and Anne Austin "arrived in the road before Boston before ever a law was made there against Quakers," Sewel says, "and yet they were very ill treated." They were searched before they landed, and about one hundred books taken

[1] Appendix: A Quaker's Sea Journal.

from their trunks and chests and burned by the hangman. They were then committed to jail as Quakers, because one of them in speaking to the deputy governor, Richard Bellingham, said *thee* instead of *you*, which he asserted was proof enough. They were stripped and searched under pretence of finding some evidence of witchcraft, and kept without light, the windows being boarded up to prevent any communication with them. Nor was any food provided for them till Nicholas Upsal " was so concerned about it (liberty being denied to send them provisions) that he purchased it of the jailor at the rate of five shillings a week, lest they should have starved." After five weeks of this treatment, a shipmaster was bound in one hundred pounds' bond to carry them back to England, and the jailor kept their beds and their Bibles for his fee. Scarcely a month after the arrival of these two fearless women, eight more Friends arrived, and were treated in the same manner, and sent back after eleven weeks in the Boston jail.[1]

It was at this juncture that Robert Fowler came to London with his offer of the new ship, and found five of the Friends who

[1] Sewel's *History*, vol. i. pp. 210, 211.

had been sent back from Boston determined to go once more. Six other Friends joined them, and the little company made ready to sail from Southampton. The captain's mind almost failed him, but, encouraged by George Fox, he writes: " I received the Lord's servants on board, who came with them, with a mighty hand and an outstretched arm." Fowler has left an account of this voyage, called " A True Relation of the Voyage undertaken by me, Robert Fowler, with my small veffel called the 'Woodhoufe;' but performed by the Lord, like as he did Noah's Ark, wherein he shut up a few righteous perfons, and landed them safe even at the hill of Ararat." Besides Fowler, the master, the crew consisted of only two men and three boys, and he declares that they made none of the usual observations, but waited daily upon the Lord, for "we see the Lord leading our veffel even as it were a man leading a horse by the head." The voyage took two months, and our respect for Fowler's seamanship is justified by the fact that New Amsterdam was the first port they sighted. Here they landed five passengers, while with the remaining six the Woodhouse proceeded to

Rhode Island, or, as we should now say, Newport, where "we were received with much joy of heart," one of the Friends writes.

Mary Clark was one of these passengers, who had left her husband, a merchant tailor in London, with her children, and went to Boston "to warn these persecutors to desist from their iniquity; but after she had delivered her message, she was unmercifully rewarded with twenty stripes of a whip with three cords, on her naked back, and detained prisoner about twelve weeks in the winter season. The cords of these whips," Sewel adds, "were commonly as thick as a man's little finger, having each some knots at the end; and the stick was sometimes so long that the hangman made use of both his hands to strike the harder."

Christopher Holder and John Copeland, passengers on the Woodhouse, who had been banished from Boston the previous year, also pushed their way into the colony. Holder endeavored to speak a few words at Salem "after the priest was done," but was hauled out of church by the hair of his head, and a glove and handkerchief thrust into his mouth. From Salem he was sent to Boston, where whipping and cruel imprisonment awaited him.

Thus early did the passengers of the Woodhouse bear testimony against the tyrannical laws in the Massachusetts.

Mary Fisher, one of the two first Friends who came, had an experience of more Christian treatment from the Mohammedan sultan a few years later, when in 1660 she journeyed in the East, and at Adrianople went " alone into the camp and got somebody to go to the tent of the grand vizier to tell him an English woman was come who had something to declare from the great God to the sultan." He procured an audience for her the next morning, and coming to the camp alone as before, she was received as became an ambassador. She hesitated to speak, " mightily pondering what she might say," when the sultan inquired " if she desired that any might go aside," and when she answered no, " bade her speak the word of the Lord to them and not to fear, for they had good hearts and could hear it." The Turks listened with respect till she had done, and the sultan said she had spoken the truth. He desired her to stay in the country, " saying that they could not but respect such a one as should take so much pains to come to them so far as from England with a message from the Lord God." He offered her a guard to conduct her to Constantinople, which she refused, though the sultan pressed it upon her, saying it was in respect to her, for he would not she should come to the least hurt in his dominions. But she persisted in declining it, and arrived in Constantinople " without the least hurt or scoff," and returned safe to England.[1]

What a contrast to the return to England from New England, only four years before, after public whipping and untold indignities, and all manner of hardship!

Sarah Gibbons and Dorothy Waugh, also of the Woodhouse company, bore public testimony in Boston, and it was of William Brand, of that same heroic company, that John Norton said, when he lay almost dead after repeated and cruel whippings, " W. Brand endeavored to beat our gospel ordinances black and blue, if then he be beaten black and blue it is but just upon him; and I will appear in his behalf that did so." This Norton added because the people were

[1] Sewel's *History*, vol. i. p. 328.

exasperated at this cruelty, and "caused such a cry that the governor sent his surgeon to the prison to see what might be done."[1]

Sewel's History, in which these things are recorded, was written by a Dutchman, a learned Quaker of Amsterdam, whose grandfather was one of the Englishmen who left home for conscience' sake. His knowledge of Greek, Latin, English, French, and High Dutch was acquired "while throwing the shuttle in the loom, during his apprenticeship to a stuff maker." He wrote a dictionary and grammar of his own language, and translated many treatises. His "History of the Rise, Increase and Progress of the Christian People called Quakers" was written in Low Dutch, and translated by himself into English. The first English edition was published in 1722 in London. " I do not pretend to elegancy in the English tongue," he says, "for being a foreigner and never having been in England but about the space of ten months, and that nearly fifty years ago, it ought not to be expected that I should write English so well as Dutch, my native tongue." But his Eng-

[1] Sewel, *History*, vol. i. p. 254.

lish needs little apology. It is direct, simple, and forcible, perhaps far better than if he had attempted the "elegancy" of his time. The documents he has preserved are invaluable, and his own comments so apposite that his work is the standard authority to-day on the history of Friends, no less than when it was published. Longfellow studied it so closely for his New England Tragedy of John Endicott, that whole passages are simply paraphrases from Sewel, as, for instance, this speech of Norton's : —

"Now hear me,
This William Brand of yours has tried to beat
Our Gospel Ordinances black and blue;
And, if he has been beaten in like manner,
It is but justice, and I will appear
In his behalf that did so."

The zeal of Endicott, and "priest Norton," as Sewel calls him, for the suppression of heresy, is too well known to require setting forth in this place. It must be remembered what times they lived in, and the fact that their theology practically made the world, not God's world, but the devil's. Thus many seriously believed that, in coming to a new country inhabited by heathen, they were come to the territory of Satan, and consequently had to fight the powers of darkness with every weapon possible. The laws of the colony of New Plymouth contain among the "offences capitall," under which head wilful murder, burning of houses and ships, with gross offences against morality, are classed, an offence which is described as a " Solemn Compaction or conversing with the divell by way of witchcraft conjuracõn or the like." A community which conceived it possible for persons to make this " Solemn Compaction" could not be expected to judge leniently opinions differing from their own. Under the theocratic theory of government, the civil arm was bound to attend to morals, and what was a more deadly sin than heresy? The special offences of the Quakers were set forth in an act made at a General Court held at Boston the 20th of October, 1658, in which the legislation of two years against the Quakers culminated. Following acts which provided for whipping and the cutting off of ears, this act of 1658 provided for the arrest without warrant of any Quaker by any constable or selectman, who should commit the Quaker to close jail without bail, until the next court, when he should be tried, and, being proved a Quaker, should be banished on pain of death. A legal trial was, by a law made in the same year, adjudged to be a trial by a court of three magistrates without jury, who had power to hang at pleasure. This law was made by so small a majority, only one vote Sewel says, that the magistrates were constrained to add, " to be tried by special jury." Longfellow sums up the legislation very accurately in " John Endicott " : —

> " Whereas a cursed set of Heretics
> Has lately risen commonly called Quakers,
> Who take upon themselves to be commissioned
> Immediately from God, and furthermore
> Infallibly assisted by the Spirit
> To write and utter blasphemous opinions,
> Despising Government and the order of God
> In church and commonwealth and speaking evil
> Of Dignities, reproaching and reviling
> The Magistrates and Ministers, and seeking
> To turn the people from their faith, and thus
> Gain proselytes to their pernicious ways ; —
> This court considering the premises,
> And to prevent like mischief which is wrought
> By their means in our land, doth hereby order
> That whatsoever master or commander
> Of any ship, bark, pink or catch shall bring
> To any roadstead, harbor, creek or cove
> Within this jurisdiction any Quakers
> Or other blasphemous Heretics, shall pay
> Unto the Treasurer of the Commonwealth
> One hundred pounds, and in default thereof

>Be put in prison and continue there
>Till the said sum be satisfied and paid."
>
>. . . . . .
>
>"If any one within this jurisdiction
>Shall henceforth entertain, or shall conceal
>Quakers, or other blasphemous Heretics,
>Knowing them so to be, every such person
>Shall forfeit to the country forty shillings
>For each hour's entertainment or concealment,
>And shall be sent to prison, as aforesaid,
>Until the forfeiture be wholly paid."
>
>. . . . . .
>
>"And it is further ordered and enacted,
>If any Quaker, or Quakers, shall presume
>To come henceforth into this jurisdiction,
>Every male Quaker for the first offence
>Shall have one ear cut off; and shall be kept
>At labor in the Workhouse till such time
>As he be sent away at his own charge.
>And for the repetition of the offence
>Shall have his other ear cut off, and then
>Be branded in the palm of his right hand.
>And every woman Quaker shall be whipt
>Severely in three towns; and every Quaker,
>Or he or she, that shall for a third time
>Herein again offend, shall have their tongues
>Bored through with a hot iron, and shall be
>Sentenced to Banishment on pain of death."

Nor did these cruel laws end here, for the magistrates were alive to the disapproval of the larger minded of the people, as Nicholas Upsall, who sent food to the starving Quakeresses, found to his cost. A clause was added for the special benefit of such men.

"Every inhabitant of this Jurisdiction
Who shall defend the horrible opinions
Of Quakers, by denying due respect
To equals and superiors, and withdrawing
From Church Assemblies, and thereby approving
The abusive and destructive practices
Of this accursed sect, in opposition
To all the orthodox received opinions
Of godly men, shall be forthwith committed
Unto close prison for one month; and then
Refusing to retract and to reform
The opinions as aforesaid, he shall be
Sentenced to Banishment on pain of Death.
By the Court. Edward Rawson, Secretary."

Nicholas Upsall could not forbear to protest against the early laws, for Longfellow's summary covers two years' legislation, and warned the magistrates, not only of the unreasonableness of their proceedings, but to take care they be not found fighting against God. But this was taken so ill that he was fined, and imprisoned for not coming to church, and finally banished in the winter season.

"Coming at length to Rhode Island, he met an Indian prince," Sewel says, "who having understood how he had been dealt with, behaved himself very kindly, and told him, if he would live with him, he would make him a warm house, and further said, 'What a God have the English, who deal so with one another about their God!'"

Notwithstanding the severity of these laws, or rather because of their severity, Quakers continued to come to Massachusetts. When the seaboard was closely guarded against them, they found entrance by "a back door," as Edward Rawson, the Secretary of the Colony, declares to the King and Council in 1661. The penalties were proved insufficient "to restrain their impudent and insolent obtrusions," and he goes on to describe the measures taken as "a defence against their impetuous, frantic fury," which "necessitated us to endeavor our security." We have already seen that Rhode Island was the "back door" through which these "malignant promoters of doctrines directly tending to subvert both church and state" found entrance into the well-guarded colony. The worst of the offences against civil government seems to have been the failure to doff the hat to a magistrate. Some of the women bore testimony against the cruel laws by wearing sackcloth, with ashes on their heads, or declared the spiritual nakedness of the rulers by a visible exemplification. But in a time when it was no uncommon thing to see a woman, stripped to the waist, fastened to the tail of a cart, and whipped in the centre of the town by the public hangman by the magistrates' order, these voluntary testimonies are the less surprising. "It must be admitted," Whittier writes of these early Friends, "that many of them manifested a good deal of that wild enthusiasm which has always been the result of persecution, and the denial of the rights of conscience and worship."

But Quakers simply travelling from one place to another, with no other offence than being Quakers, were unsafe. Hored Gardner, who is described as an inhabitant of Newport, came to Weymouth, "with her sucking babe, and a girl to carry it," in 1658, "whence for being a Quaker she was hurried to Boston, where both she and the girl were whipped with a three-fold knot. After whipping, the woman kneeled down, and prayed the Lord to forgive those persecutors; which so touched a woman that stood by, that she said, surely she could not have done this if it had not been by the spirit of the Lord."

The most famous case of suffering among

the early Friends was that of Mary Dyer. Her husband, William Dyre, as the record spells it, was a man of importance in Rhode Island. He was one of the men appointed to lay out the town of Newport, and from 1640 to 1643 was Secretary of the Colony. He held the office of General Recorder later, and was General Attorney in 1650. Mary Dyer was a woman of strong character, great enthusiasm, and excellent understanding. Sewel gives the history of her courage at length. She came to Boston from Rhode Island in 1657, he says, not knowing the laws which had been made against Quakers, and was imprisoned. William Dyer, her husband, upon hearing this, came from Rhode Island and obtained her release, "becoming bound in a great penalty not to lodge her in any town of that colony, nor permit any to speak with her: an evident token that he was not of the Society of Quakers so called, for otherwise he would not have entered into such a bond; but then without question he would also have been clapped up in prison," the worthy Dutch historian adds. Two years later (in 1659) Mary Dyer was again in Boston, when William Robinson, a merchant of

London, and Marmaduke Stevenson, came there. Nicholas Davis was also there, and after whipping Robinson, who was a teacher among the Quakers, all four were banished on pain of death. The sentence is dated September 12, 1659, and it appearing, " by their own confession, words, and actions, that they are Quakers," they are sentenced " to depart this jurisdiction on pain of death, and that they must answer it at their peril, if they or any of them after the 14th of this present month, September, are found within this jurisdiction, or any part thereof." Mary Dyer and Davis accordingly left Boston and the colony, while the others only went to Salem, not being free in mind to comply. And it was not long that Mary Dyer remained away, for in the next month (October) she returned, and all three were taken into custody. On the 20th of the month these three were brought into court, when Endicott made them an oration, declaring that the court desired not the death of any, but ending, " Give ear, and harken to your sentence of death." Robinson had prepared a paper expressly declaring that while in Rhode Island he was commanded of the Lord to repair to Boston, and lay down his life there, as a testimony against the wicked and unjust laws. This paper Endicott read, but refused to have read publicly. Stevenson was then called, and, seeing how his companion had fared, made no defence. He was sentenced to death, and it was the turn of Mary Dyer, "to whom Endicott spoke thus: 'Mary Dyer, you shall go to the place whence you came (to wit the prison) and thence to the place of execution, and be hanged there until you are dead.' To which she replied, ' The will of the Lord be done.' Then Endicott said, 'Take her away, Marshal.' To which she returned, ' Yea, joyfully I go.' And in her going to the prison, she often uttered speeches of praise to the Lord ; and being full of joy, she said to the Marshal, he might let her alone, for she would go to the prison without him. To which he answered, 'I believe you, Mrs. Dyer; but I must do what I am commanded.'"

In prison Mary Dyer wrote a very remarkable letter, addressed to the General Court in Boston, justifying her coming to Boston, as it was by the will of the Lord she came. " I have no self-ends, the Lord knoweth," she writes. Seeing the evil of their unjust laws, she entreats the court not to be found fighting against God, but "to repeal all such laws, that the Truth and servants of the Lord may have free passage among you. . . . Seeing the Lord hath not hid it from me, it lyeth upon me in love to your souls thus to persuade you. . . . Was ever the like laws heard of among a people that confess Christ come in the flesh? and have ye no other weapons to fight against spiritual wickedness withal, as you call it? Woe is me for you! Of whom take ye counsel? Search with the light of Christ in you, and it will show you of whom, as it hath done me, and many more, who have been disobedient and deceived, as now ye are; which light as ye come into, and obeying what is made manifest to you therein, you will not repent that you were kept from shedding blood, though it were by a woman." She likens her request to Esther's before Ahasuerus, saying that he did not contend it would be dishonorable to revoke his decree. She appeals to "the faithful and true witness of God which is one in all consciences. If they put this request from them, she continues, the Lord will send more of his servants to gather the harvest; for the light of the Lord is surely approaching, even to many in and about Boston, which is the bitterest and darkest professing place . . . that ever I heard of. Let the time past, therefore, suffice, for such a profession as brings forth such fruits as these laws are. In love and in the spirit of meekness I again beseech you."

Mary Dyer's query as to whether the General Court had " no other weapons to fight against spiritual wickedness withal," reminds one of the Rhode Island way of dealing with doctrine. Roger Williams stoutly maintained the " freedom of different consciences from inforcements," but he was far from indifferent as to his neighbors' beliefs. How could he be, being a godly man, and certain that by belief, rather than by conduct, a soul is to be judged? There were long discussions in Rhode Island, debates on all conceivable questions, and pamphlets appealing to the reason and conscience of the reader. These " weapons " were always at hand in the Providence plantations, and doubtless were well known to Mary Dyer. Her appeal to the General Court, written as she supposed on the eve of her execution, is certainly a noble one. From her point of view, she could have done no less than offer up her life, if the offering should secure liberty to her oppressed brethren. It is difficult to see just why she supposed it would do so. Something of stubbornness must have crept into her constancy to make her persist in sacrifice.

Her letter had small effect on the court, as may be imagined, and the day came for execution. It was the 27th of October, 1659, when the three prisoners were led to the gallows, in the afternoon, escorted by about two hundred armed men, beside horsemen, and the minister, John Wilson. The three friends walked hand in hand, Mary Dyer in the middle. As she was an elderly woman, the Marshal said to her, " Are you not ashamed to walk thus, hand in hand between two young men?" "No," replied she; " this is to me an hour of the greatest joy I could enjoy in the whole world. No eye can see, no tongue can utter, and no heart can understand the sweet incomes or influences, and the refreshings of the spirit of the Lord which I now feel;" so " they went on with great cheerfulness, as going to an everlasting wedding feast," though the drummers drowned their voices.

At the gallows Wilson made a taunting remark to Robinson: " Shall such jacks as you are come before authority with their hats on?" he asked, and Robinson replied, " Mind you, mind you, it is for not putting off the hat we are put to death." He was the first to suffer. " I suffer for Christ," he said, " in whom I live, and for whom I die." Stevenson was next hanged, with a word of holy confidence upon his lips, and Mary Dyer stepped up the ladder. The halter was adjusted, " her coats were tied about her feet," the old record says, and John Wilson lent the hangman a handkerchief to cover her face. Just as the hangman was about to do his work a cry came, "' Stop, for she is reprieved!' Her feet being then loosed, they bade her come down. But she, whose mind was already as it were in heaven, stood still and said she was there willing to suffer as her brethren did, unless they would annul their wicked law." But they pulled her down and carried her back to prison. It now appears that this was a ghastly farce arranged by the authorities to intimidate this intrepid woman. The decree itself, signed before she left the prison, prescribes the cruel method of her release. She was to be carried " to the place of execution and there to stand upon the gallowes with a rope about her necke till the rest be executed, and then to return to the prison."[1]

It was at the entreaty of her son that this reprieve was granted; "an inconsiderable intercession," the Secretary, Edward Rawson, says, in his account to the king of these proceedings. " Mary Dyer (upon petition of her son, and the mercy and clemancy of this court) had liberty to depart within two days, which she accepted of," Rawson declares. From prison, the next day after the execution, at which she manifested such heroic courage, she wrote another letter to the General Court, full of the same spirit. " When I heard your last order read, it was a disturbance unto me, that was so freely offering up my life to him that gave it me." She warns the judges to put away the evil of their doings, to " kiss the Son, the light in you, before his wrath be kindled in you." And this she wrote while the image of her dead compan-

[1] Horatio Rogers, *Mary Dyer, the Quaker Martyr*, p. 53.

ions must still have been before her eyes, and the tale of the barbarous treatment of their dead bodies in her ears. But she returned to prison, she says, " finding nothing from the Lord to the contrary, that I may know what his pleasure and counsel is concerning me, on whom I wait therefore, for he is my life and the length of my days; and as I said before, I came at his command and go at his command."

The discontent among the people was so great that the magistrates resolved to send Mary Dyer away. She was accordingly put on horseback, and escorted by four horsemen fifteen miles toward Rhode Island, where she was left with a horse and a man to complete the journey. She spent the winter in Long Island, and then, coming home in the spring, she was moved " to return to the bloody town of Boston," where she arrived on the " twenty-first of the Third month, 1660," — that is, May, for the old style of reckoning the year from the first of March was still in use. Ten days after her arrival she was sent for by the General Court. " Are you the same Mary Dyer that was here before?" Endicott asked her, and it seems the court was preparing an escape for her, being disinclined to proceed to extremities, for another Mary Dyer had come from England. But she replied undauntedly, and without evasion, " I am the same Mary Dyer that was here at the last General Court." She was then asked if she avowed herself a Quaker, to which she replied : " I own myself to be reproachfully so called." Endicott said her sentence had been passed, and was now the same. " You must return to prison," he said, " and there remain till to-morrow at nine o'clock, then, thence you must go to the gallows and there be hanged till you are dead." " This is no more than what thou saidst before," Mary Dyer rejoined. " But now it is to be executed, therefore prepare yourself to-morrow at nine o'clock," Endicott replied.

She then said, " I came in obedience to the will of God to the last General Court, desiring you to repeal your unrighteous laws of banishment on pain of death ; and that same is my work now, and earnest request," and more she said of her call, and of others who would come to witness against these laws. Endicott asked her if she were a prophetess, to which she replied that she spoke the words the Lord spoke in her, but Endicott cried out, "Away with her! away with her!" So she was taken to prison.

A letter from her husband arrived about the time Mary Dyer entered the colony, being under sentence of banishment on pain of death. "If her zeal be so great as thus to adventure, oh, let your pity and favor surmount it and save her life," her husband pleads.

I only say this, yourſelves have been, and are or may be, huſbands to wives: so am I, yea to one moſt dearly beloved. Oh do not deprive me of her, but I pray give her me once again. Pity me! I beg it with tears, and reſt your humble suppliant.[1]

But this touching appeal was of no avail. The next day, June 1st, the Marshal came and roughly commanded Mary Dyer to follow him. Then she was brought out, and with a band of soldiers led through the town, with drums beaten before and behind her. What a scene for the quiet streets of a New England town! The fresh leaves of early summer upon the trees, the sun shining overhead, the whole popula-

[1] Bryant's *History*, vol. ii. p. 194.

tion following the soldiers, the noisy drums rattling discordant notes, and the centre of of it all one lonely woman, " of a comly and grave countenance," and the undaunted carriage of a pure and lofty spirit, calmly walking to the fate which she had once before confronted, and which even now by a word from her could be averted! For after she had ascended the ladder it was said to her that if she would return she should be spared. " Nay I cannot," she replied, " for in obedience to the will of the Lord I came, and in his will I abide faithful to the death." Then the captain, John Webb, said that she had been there before, and was therefore guilty of her own death, knowing the penalty of returning to Boston; to which she replied : —

Nay, I came to keep blood guiltinefs from you, defiring you to repeal the unrighteous and unjuft law of banifhment upon pain of death, made againft the innocent servants of the Lord; therefore my blood will be required at your hands who wilfully do it; but for thofe who do it in the simplicity of their hearts I defire the Lord to forgive them.

Then Wilson, the minister, who had lent

his handkerchief to cover her face before, said to her, " Mary Dyer, oh repent, oh repent, and be not so deluded and carried away by the deceit of the devil." One can fancy the touch of scorn which must have tinged her manner, saintly as she was, as she replied, " Nay, man, I am not now to repent."

Then she was asked if she would not have the elders pray for her, but answered, " I know never an elder here."

They asked if she would have any of the people pray for her, to which she replied she desired the prayers of all the people of God. Some one scoffingly said, " It may be she thinks there is none here." And she, looking calmly about, said, " I know but few here." The prayers of the elders were again urged upon her. " Nay," she said, " first a child, then a young man, then a strong man, before an elder in Christ Jesus."

Then some one mentioned that she said she had been in paradise. " Yea, I have been in paradise several days," she answered, and continued to speak of the eternal happiness she was to enter upon. So she met her death, and died, as her chronicler says, "a martyr to Christ, being twice led to death, which the first time she expected with undaunted courage, and now suffered with Christian fortitude."

I have dwelt at length upon the story of Mary Dyer's heroic courage, because she was the only woman who suffered death in that time of persecution, and because she was a Rhode Island woman, closely bound by ties of love and friendship to the Friends already in Rhode Island.

At this distance of time, we can see that the magistrates also had something to plead as warrant for their conduct. She had been warned, and in coming back took her life in her hand. The dignity of the law had to be upheld. We have had cases in more recent times of unjust laws being enforced, by judges who did not believe in them, in the very town of Boston, in the time of the fugitive slaves. There was something in their argument that her blood was upon her own head. But with the spirit of a saint she rose above all human argument. Like a Hebrew of old she could say, "The word of the Lord came unto me;" and with St. Paul, "Woe is me if I preach not the gospel." This zeal consumed her.

Quaker though she was, and so bound to meekness by teaching and principle, she had tasted the glories of martyrdom, and could not rest till she was counted worthy to suffer to the end. If, in our modern spirit, we inquire what her husband and children said to her sacrifice not only of herself but of them, and the suffering and pain she brought them, her grave face, with its rapt expression, rises to rebuke us. This life was nothing, the next all, in those stern, heroic times. Earthly affections were to be trodden under foot. "Set your affections on things above" was an injunction to be literally followed. So, with a responsive thrill for her noble courage, and a sigh for the occasion of it, we finish the record of this heroic woman. Her death reaped its harvest. The "Seed," as Friends delighted to call the principles of truth they lived and died for, flourished abundantly. Within a year of Mary Dyer's death, the Rhode Island yearly meeting was established, which grew till it became the general meeting for the whole of New England.

II
THE ESTABLISHMENT OF THE SOUTH KINGSTON MONTHLY MEETING

1

II

THE little colony which proved a refuge for Quakers not only, but for all those of oppressed conscience, had only been united as to civil government three years, when the Woodhouse landed her missionary band on the "isle of Aquiday." There were political dissensions as well as religious. After the charter had been granted to Roger Williams, in 1643, it was still four years before the towns united in setting "their hands to an engagement to the charter;"[1] a delay caused in part by the difficulties of travel, and the long voyage from England. The two island towns of Newport and Portsmouth were richer than the little towns of Providence and Warwick, and local jealousies were rife. Governor Coddington of Newport, in 1651, obtained a commission as governor for life, "whereby the Townes of Newport and Portsmouth were disjoynted from the Colonie of Providence Plantations,"[2] and it

[1] R. I. C. R., vol. i. p. 147.
[2] R. I. C. R., vol. i. p. 268.

was not till August 31, 1654, that the final union of the towns was accomplished.

With this disordered political condition, the religious conditions were still more disturbed. The disaffected from all the colonies came to Rhode Island. All varieties and shades of opinions could be found, from harmless mysticism to doctrines subversive of the good order of society, and many a wild theory was propounded. Rhode Island has often been spoken of as a colony of religious toleration. But it was not toleration that Roger Williams taught. He laid down a larger principle, the "freedom of different consciences from inforcement," that is, the broad principle of each man's being the sole arbiter of his own fate, and directly responsible to his Maker for his belief. This was a new doctrine, a doctrine of growth and development, calculated to build strong and noble characters. But, while remaining true to it, Roger Williams did not weakly shake off all responsibility as to the spiritual condition of his colonists. On the contrary, while keeping clear from the "inforcements" which were so freely used in the neighboring colonies, he gave full rein to his tongue, using all the weapons of argument and invective to scourge the wayward fanatics who came to him back into what he considered the true way. The story has often been told, and needs no repeating here. Whittier, with true insight, has entered into Roger Williams's feeling, in " A Spiritual Manifestation," when he makes him say: —

> " Each zealot thrust before my eyes
>   His Scripture-garbled label;
> All creeds were shouted in my ears
>   As with the tongues of Babel.
>
> . . . .
>
> " Hoarse ranters, crazed Fifth Monarchists
>   Of stripes and bondage braggarts,
> Pale Churchmen, with singed rubrics snatched
>   From Puritanic fagots.
>
> " And last, not least, the Quakers came,
>   With tongues still sore from burning,
> The Bay State's dust from off their feet
>   Before my threshold spurning;
>
> " A motley host, the Lord's *débris*,
>   Faith's odds and ends together;
> Well might I shrink from guests with lungs
>   Tough as their breeches leather:
>
> . . . .
>
> " I fed, but spared them not a wit;
>   I gave to all who walked in,
> Not clams and succotash alone,
>   But stronger meat of doctrine.

"I proved the prophets false, I pricked
The bubble of perfection,
And clapped upon their inner light
The snuffers of election."

It was in this country of "faith's odds and ends" that the Quakers found their opportunity. The martyrdom of Mary Dyer watered the seed, and when George Fox came, twelve years later, he confirmed the church. The visit of Fox was the starting point for many meetings in America, but in coming to Rhode Island he came to his own. He arrived on the 30th of the 3d month, 1672, from Long Island, and was "gladly received by Friends," he writes. This was the 30th of May that he arrived, when he "went to Nicholas Eastons, who was governor of the Island; there we lay, being weary with travelling." He had a meeting the next first day, a large meeting, he says, "to which the deputy governor and several justices came, and were mightily affected with the truth." It is curious to note how often Fox mentions the dignitaries who attended his meetings, in spite of his being no respecter of persons. The week following his arrival, the June yearly meeting for Friends in New

England was held. Fox himself tells the story of it. Some Barbadoes friends arrived; and the meeting lasted six days, he says, and —

Abundance of other people came. For having no prieſts in the iſland, and no reſtriction to any particular way of worship; and the governor and deputy-governor with several juſtices of the peace daily frequenting meetings; it so encouraged the people that they flocked in from all parts of the iſland. . . . I have rarely obſerved a people in the state wherein they stood, to hear with more attention, diligence, and affection, than generally they did during the four days.

Men's and women's meetings followed for " ordering the affairs of the church, . . . that all might be kept clean, sweet and savory amongſt them." After which Friends dispersed. But Fox and Robert Widders stayed on the island, " finding service still here for the Lord through the great openness, and the daily coming in of freſh people from other colonies for some time after the general meeting." " After this I had great travail in spirit," he writes, " concerning the Ranters in those parts who had been rude at a meeting which I was not at." So he appointed a meeting among them, "believing the Lord would give me power over them; which he did to his praise and glory." At this meeting also there were justices and officers who were "generally well affected with the truth." One justice of twenty years' standing was convinced, "spoke highly of the truth, and more highly of me," Fox adds, "than is fit for me to mention or take notice of." What comfort it must have been to the travelling Friend, who was usually greeted with stripes and imprisonment in his own country, to find true appreciation! His chief acquaintance with justices in England was as a prisoner on charge of breaking the peace, and it is small wonder that, saint as he was, this being heard with favor by justices and officers should have seemed to him a special cause for thanksgiving.

After the Newport meetings, Fox went to Providence in great travail of spirit, for the people, he says, "were generally above the priests in high notions; and some came on purpose to dispute." There had been absolute freedom in the little town of

Providence in the thirty-six years of its existence. Each householder could, and often did, exhort. Roger Williams, with the humility of greatness, counted himself only as a teacher also; one among many. But the power of George Fox's eloquence and personality silenced his opponents. He came from Newport by water, attended by the governor and many others, and held his meeting in a great barn, which was thronged with people, "so that I was exceeding hot, and in a great sweat," he writes; "but all was well; the glorious power of the Lord shined over all!"

Roger Williams was not at the meeting that hot summer's day, but a little later rowed himself to Newport to confront the advocates of the Quaker doctrine. He and Fox did not meet, however. One wonders if they could have recognized the nobility of each other's nature had they seen each other face to face, or if the "Burrows" from which Roger Williams "digg^d George Fox[1]" were too dark and mystical for the scientific spirit of Williams to tolerate. There must always be the two orders of men,—the intuitive seer, and the logical reasoner. Both

[1] *George Fox digg^d out of his Burrows.*

these men have their noble share of the world's work, and in the case of Fox and Williams both made a distinct contribution to the spiritual life of mankind; Fox with his devout and keen perception of divine immanence in the indwelling spirit, and Williams with his new doctrine of the freedom of man's conscience from "inforcements." These two should certainly have found points of contact in an age which is the fruit of both their teachings. As it was, the apostle came to the town of the liberator, and left it without seeing him. After the manner of the time, they both wrote polemical tracts, the most famous of which is Williams's "George Fox digg^d out of his Burrows."

Returning to Newport, Fox next went across the Bay to Narragansett. Again the governor accompanied him, and they held a meeting at a justice's, "where Friends never had any before." I have elsewhere endeavored to show that this meeting was probably held at the house of Jireh Bull,[1] who was a justice at that time. The year before, the General Court sat at his house. It was sometimes called the garrison house,

[1] *College Tom*, p. 9. Houghton, Mifflin & Co.

and was the largest in Pettaquamscut. "The meeting was very large, for the country generally came in, and people from Connecticut and other parts round about,"[1] Fox writes. "There were four justices of the peace," he adds. "Most of these people were such as had never heard Friends before; but they were mightily affected, and a great desire there is after the truth amongst them. So that meeting was of very good service; blessed be the Lord forever!" The justice at whose house the meeting was held invited Fox to come again, but he was then "clear of those parts." But he laid the place before John Burnyeate and John Cartwright, who arrived in Newport before he left, and they "felt drawings thither and went to visit them."

The house in which this Narragansett meeting was established had a tragic fate. It stood on the old Pequot trail, which in Queen Anne's time became the highway, on the ridge of Tower Hill. Tradition places it on the right-hand side travelling north, a little distance south of the present corner made by the descent of the road

[1] *Journal*, p. 452.

running to the west. Only three years later, in December, 1675, it was destroyed by Indians, and many of its inmates, including women and children, were killed. It was the destruction of this house which was the actual incitement to the Great Swamp Fight, which practically exterminated the Indians, and put an end to King Philip's War.

There are no records of Friends' meetings on the west side of the Bay until 1702, when the Greenwich meeting was established, which included the Narragansett Friends. This at first sight seems singular, for Narragansett, and southern Narragansett, had been the place of Fox's visit, and was occupied by some influential converts.

But there were good reasons why the King's Province could not establish a meeting in those early days. The country was claimed by charter right by both Connecticut and Rhode Island, and endless controversies ensued as to the government. But in addition to this, the land was claimed by two rival purchasers ; the Pettaquamscut purchasers, who bought Boston Neck and lands adjacent of the Indians in 1657, and the Humphrey Atherton Company, who bought "two parsels of lande," called the Northern and Southern tract, in 1659. This land covered the land of the earlier purchase, including Point Juda and Sugar Loaf Hill.[1] Both these companies had the Indian "sagamores" put their marks to the deeds of purchase, which they naturally had little conception of. This is not the place for a study of the interesting and extended controversy which ensued. But a glance at the men who were engaged in it, and who claimed the right of proprietors in the land, will explain why Friends for some years did not set up a meeting in Narragansett. Among the Pettaquamscut purchasers, Samuel Sewall soon became a leading spirit. He was an example of the best Puritans of his time, but his action in the trial of the Salem witches shows the bigotry to which the best men were liable. Of the other company, the man who gave it its name, Major Humphrey Atherton, or Adderton, as some records spell it, was active in his persecution of Quakers. Simon Bradstreet was another zealous bigot. The younger Winthrop, governor of Connecticut, was

[1] *The Town Records*, edited by James N. Arnold.

far more liberal, and his name, as the highest in rank, comes first in the deeds, but his influence in the affairs of the company was second to Atherton's. It is hardly probable that zealous persecutors at home would have tolerated Quaker organizations in the new purchase, which they hoped to develop into a prosperous colony. It was Atherton who scoffed at the death of Mary Dyer, saying she hung as a flag for others to take warning by. Long after her death, in passing the place where Quakers suffered, as he rode proudly by, having reviewed his troops, his horse took fright and threw him violently, dashing his head in pieces. There were not lacking those who said the animal saw the ghost of one of the martyrs, and that their death was avenged. But even after Atherton's tragic end, Simon Bradstreet's name would have held in check the open organization of a meeting.

That the meeting was held, however, would seem to be indicated from several facts. It was in 1699 that the Rhode Island quarterly meeting was established, consisting of three monthly meetings, Rhode Island, Dartmouth, and Narragansett. This last meeting was at first called Kingstown meeting, but very soon changed to Greenwich, and included all the Friends on the west side of the Bay, from Narragansett to Providence. A little meeting-house was built in East Greenwich in 1699, the first one on the west of the Bay, meetings having been held before at private houses. The records of the Greenwich monthly meeting begin in 5th month, 1699 (the day is obliterated), at the house of John Briggs, when it was agreed that he " write for these meetings." A month later the meeting was held at Jabez Greene's house, and on the 5th of sixth month of the same year the " next meeting is appointed to be held at the new meeting house in East Greenwich."

This little meeting-house was built to the west of the village, and had a burial-ground adjoining. It was the first meeting-house west of Narragansett Bay; and here the meetings were held, not only the first-day meeting for worship, but the monthly meetings, to which representatives came from South Kingstown, Providence, and Warwick. In 1707 the meetings began to be held in rotation, three yearly at Providence and three at Kingstown. This arrangement continued till 1718, when Providence became a distinct monthly meeting. South Kingstown Friends still came to Greenwich for monthly meeting. Rowland Robinson, John Briggs, Peter Greene, the Knowleses and Rodmans were among the representatives of the southern part of the State. It was a time of great prosperity for Narragansett. The farms yielded bountifully; the ferry to Newport was crowded with droves of sheep and cattle going to market, and produce of all kinds. The tide of travel was all set across the Bay rather than to the head of the Bay, and before many years Narragansett Friends petitioned for a separate meeting. It was at the third month monthly meeting, 1743, when Thomas Rodman and Matthew Allin (*sic*) were representatives from South Kingstown, that an epistle from the quarterly meeting was read at Greenwich, which allowed the meeting to be divided into two monthly meetings. The record continues : —

This meeting concludes that the monthly meeting is divided into two monthly meetings as the Preparative meetings were before this diviſion, and that South Kingſtown monthly meeting be held on the 2nd day after the laſt 1st

day in this month to do the proper bufiness of that meeting in the meeting house of Friends in South Kingstown.

There is no indication as to when the " meeting house of Friends in South Kingstown " was built. For many years it was called " the old meeting house," and in 1743 it became the centre of influence and seat of government of Friends in Narragansett.

III
THE MEETING-HOUSES

III

IT was the third month, 1743, that the South Kingstown monthly meeting began its existence by the consent of the quarterly meeting and the Greenwich meeting, to which the South Kingstown preparative meeting had belonged. The first monthly meeting was appointed the following month, but the records do not begin till the fifth month, 1743. There are eight folio volumes belonging to the men's meeting, which contain the records of the business of the meeting from month to month, the list of births, marriages, and deaths, and a beautiful manuscript of the English book of discipline, which was made between 1761 and 1763. Thomas Hazard and Joseph Congdon were the committee appointed to see to this work, for which fifty pounds old tenor was paid. It is entitled "Christian & Brotherly Advices Given forth from time to time By the yearly Meeting in London. Alphabetically Digefted under Proper Heads. Tranfcribed by Jos: Congdon." Beside the records of the men's meeting, there are three volumes of women's records, — the earliest a small quarto, the others large folios. There is also a mass of papers belonging to the meeting, deeds of the meeting-house lands, epistles from quarterly meetings, beginning as early as 1747, yearly meeting epistles, and the originals of various papers copied in the records. They are a set of time-stained books and documents, the paper discolored and brittle, cracking in the folds, exhaling the peculiar breath of long-kept mustiness. The handwriting is often crabbed, the spelling eccentric, the records themselves curt and scanty. Yet here is preserved all that is left of the best life of many good men and women. The voice of their preaching has died upon the air, the savor of their virtues exists only in tradition; but the record of their actual work is preserved. The houses of worship which they built have crumbled, but the account of their labors in building remains.

It is often said we lack glamour in America, that our perspective is limited, that we have no picturesque past. But all these things lie more in the eye of the beholder than in external objects. Natural beauty is as beautiful in New England as in Old. We have no Tintern Abbey, it is true, but our greater lack is a Wordsworth to celebrate it.

> " Art was given for that;
> God uses us to help each other so,
> Lending our minds out."

It is the mind, the love, the life of man which must reveal beauty to us who have our turn at living now. Looked at in this spirit, what can be more fascinating, what can claim our interest and reverent affection, more than such a mass of records and papers as those of the Narragansett meeting? For this was life: this meant not only daily affairs, of which there is abundant evidence, but it meant the care of good men for the soul's welfare. We may have outgrown the methods; humanity cannot outgrow the aim.

Whatever those worthies truly wrought has gone into the fabric of later time. Their Narragansett lies before us, unchanged as to physical features, but more thickly peopled, with villages dotting the pleasant dales. Let us try to turn back the years to that summer day in 1743 when the first recorded meeting was held. Riding through the narrow lanes, from beyond Little Rest and up from Westerly, came the representatives to that meeting. The old meeting-house — old in 1743 — stood upon the southern spur of Tower Hill, a mile or more from the village. The first mention of this building occurs in Judge Sewall's diary, under an entry of Friday, September 20, 1706, when he went " into the Quaker Meeting Houfe, about thirty-five feet long, thirty feet wide, on Hazard's ground, which was mine."[1] The sale of this land to Thomas Hazard was made in 1698, so that it must have been a comparatively new building at the time of Sewall's visit. The South Kingstown Records have something further to say of this land. August 4, 1710, Thomas Hazard sold one acre to Ebenezer Slocum, of Jamestown, for forty shillings; and the next day it was conveyed by Slocum to Rowland Robinson, Samuel Perry, Henry Knowles, Jr., Thomas Rodman, and Jacob Mott, for the same consideration. The bounds are given, easterly and southerly by the road, the rest by Hazard's land, " being that parcel of land on which Stands a cer-

[1] *Sewall Papers*, vol. ii. p. 168.

tain Meeting House in which the people called Quakers usually meet."[1] It commanded a wide prospect of land and water. At the foot of the hill the chain of Point Judith ponds begins, which separate the Point from the mainland; and the perilous Point itself, called in the old deeds Point Juda, or Point Jude, stretches a warning finger far out into the white breakers. Block Island, the land of Manassees, lies in the distance to the southwest; while to the east the unbroken ocean stretches to the coast of Africa. Close at hand, the Pettaquamscut winds through its marshes; the crescent of Little Neck beach is white with foam; and but a little farther the windows of Newport gleam in the sunshine. A lovely prospect those "weighty" Friends had to look upon. Some of the women doubtless enjoyed it, but the appeal of natural beauty was not generally felt, and the commanding situation was doubtless chosen more in reference to the onslaught of Indians than for picturesqueness.

In this " olde meeting house " the meeting was organized. Peter Davis was chosen " to write for the meeting," — to become its

[1] *South Kingstown Records*, vol. ii.

clerk, in other words. He does not record the fact himself; it is only from a subsequent entry, when he was superseded, that it is learned. He had an interesting career, which is briefly outlined by the records, in which he constantly appears. Thomas Rodman was chosen the meeting's treasurer, and served long and well. He was called Dr. Rodman, and practised the healing art. This was perhaps the only title that the strictness of Friends admitted of; but the life of a country physician, who literally went about doing good, earned this most peaceful and honorable of titles. Books for record were bought, for which £2 14s. were paid, and the meeting entered on the difficult question of fixing its boundaries. In a new country this is always a serious task, and in no part of New England was there more difficulty than in Narragansett. As already detailed, rival governments claimed the whole country; and the inhabitants must have become accustomed to an unsettled state of affairs of this nature, for it took the sober and orderly Friends of Narragansett seventeen years to decide what was their proper jurisdiction. It was not till 1760 that a joint committee from the East Greenwich meeting and the South Kingstown meeting finally made the report " that each may know which are their proper members." The South Kingstown meeting bounds were to begin at Bissell's Mills on the north. This is now called Hamilton Mills, and lies on the shore near Wickford. From thence the boundary ran " to the Highway that leads westward to the house where Robert Eldrish formerly lived, thence by Said Highway to the Cross Highway by Nicholas Gardner's, thence a strait line to Boon's house, upon black plain, thence to the Highway in narrow Laine by James Reynolds & by said Highway to the Colony Line."[1] Black Plain and Narrow Lane have passed from remembrance, and the houses of these worthy men know them no more; but in a general way it is safe to say that the South Kingstown meeting included the whole of Washington County, and a portion of what is now Connecticut, since Stonington was evidently included within its limits.

Almost the first business which came before the meeting in the first year of its

[1] Vol. i. p. 104.

existence was the "matter of building a meeting house in the north west part of Westerly." The "Lower part of Westerly" also desired a meeting-house, one meeting-house to be ten miles distant from the other. At a meeting held in Charlestown, the 29th of 6th month, 1743, a committee report on the size of the lower meeting-house. They recommend a "Houfe of Eighteen feet one way and 26 feet another way and about 9 or ten feet Stud and about £200 money they think will accomplifh S^d Houfe."[1] A few months later Peter Davis, his sons William, and Peter Davis, Jr., were appointed "to fe to the Carrying on of Said Building."

At first sight this seems a great sum to pay for a little building of eighteen by twenty-six feet. But the currency was enormously depreciated. In 1740 it required twenty-seven shillings in bills to equal an ounce of silver, whose normal rate of exchange in the same year was six shillings ninepence.[2] So that the inflation was exactly four hundred per cent., and to get an

[1] Vol. i. p. 2.
[2] Weeden, *Economic and Social History of New England*, chap. xiii.; *R. I. Historical Tracts*, No. 8, p. 55.

idea of true value the two hundred pounds must become fifty. All the prices mentioned must be reduced as much or more, for the currency went on depreciating, until at last, in 1781, one Spanish milled dollar was equal to sixteen hundred dollars in paper!

The independent existence of the meeting seems to have acted as a stimulus in building houses of worship. It was soon under consideration to build a meeting-house in the southwest part of South Kingstown. A committee was appointed in 1748 to conclude "where to fet the meeting houfe they are about to build." Two Perrys, James and Benjamin, with three other Friends, were appointed, but the next month the proposal was "Dropt for the prefent." Friends doubtless had enough on hand at the moment, for the upper meeting-house at Westerly was reported "not yet fit to meet in in cold weather, and all the money spent." It was recommended to quarterly meeting for assistance. But the need of a house of worship was evidently great, for a Friend is dealt with for " suffering Friends to be disorderly Impofed upon in their public meeting at his houfe, and he not forbid the diforder."[1]

So the heart of James Perry was evidently moved, for in 1750 he conveyed a piece of land by deed to the meeting " to and for the ufe of ffriends to fet a Meeting houfe on, and for a burying Ground." The meeting agreed to fence the ground, and a committee was appointed to place the house and fix the size. The house was to be somewhat larger than the Westerly lower meeting-house built a few years ago. This was thirty-two by twenty-four feet, "and 9 foot and a half poft," but the " coft they fuppofe will be about £750!" So in seven years the cost for a building only one third larger increased three and one half times. This little meeting-house stood long in the "hill country" in Matunuck, back from the highway to the west of the road. Of late years it was surrounded by huckleberry pastures, whose rich russet red in the early autumn made a fitting setting for the venerable structure. To it a little company of worshipers gathered each year on a summer First Day. Here again was heard the sound of prayer and exhortation; and if the melody

[1] Vol. i. p. 30.

of hymns floated from its trembling windows, it shocked no listening Friends, for the preacher who held the service was that friend of humanity who has banded his brethren together "in His Name." By the pious care of several of these summer pilgrims, the little building was preserved until a very few years ago. One summer when they returned from a winter's absence they found it a heap of rubbish!

In spite of the disordered state of the currency, Friends kept on building; and in 1753 Richmond wished a meeting-house, to be built on the highway which leads from John Knowles's to Mumford's Mills. The dimensions were of what appears to have been the usual size, thirty-two by twenty-four feet, "and of a height for a convenient Galarie" the record adds. Four hundred and eighty-eight pounds were immediately subscribed, and the matter was referred to quarterly meeting. This house finally cost £824 5s. 5d., as the completed account shows. Only £727 18s. 6d. were received when the account was rendered, "fo that there remains due to the undertakers £96 6s. 11d., — and there is £16 1s. 6d. of the fubfcriptions unpaid." It stood within the limits of the town of Richmond, from which it took its name, to the west of Kingston, somewhat south of the present village of Usquepaug. The highway still exists as a quiet country road, and, driving westward from Kingston Depot, to the right lies a little knoll, now bare and deserted, save for a few moss-grown stones which guard the resting-places of the dead. Here the meeting-house was built. The quiet country stretches in soft undulations about it. The farms are now almost deserted; here and there a column of smoke rising from a group of old apple-trees marks a household. A few stately avenues of old trees between moss-grown walls lead to dilapidated buildings which once were fine mansions. A feeling of autumn creeps into even spring-time air, as of a land that has passed its vigorous youth, and lies basking tranquilly after days of achievement. Or is it waiting the coming of some hero of romance to wake this sleeping beauty, and once again fill the fields, now so desolate, with activity and life?

In the days of the Friends' meeting, it was a busy centre. Around the place of gathering stretched the fields of the

Hoxsies, Solomon and Stephen, both men of mark and influence in the meeting. Here the business of the Friends' meetings was transacted, alternating with those on Tower Hill and in the Westerly meeting-house. It happens that much of the important business we shall review occurred here. Here the first protest against slavery was made, and here some of the most influential of the members were brought to account for delinquencies.

Beside building its own meeting-houses, the South Kingstown meeting contributed to others, as it in turn also received contribution. Warwick, Dartmouth, and Providence each had contributions in the early days of the meeting. South Kingstown was the richest town in the colony about the middle of the century, and it is natural to find Friends contributing considerable sums. But, while Friends were generous, they were thrifty. After having contributed seventy-two pounds fifteen shillings toward various meeting-houses, especially the meeting-house at Providence, comes the entry :

" This meeting do not find freedom to contribute any more till they are Satisfied the augmenting of the firſt ſum which was

Requefted is not by unneceffary coft."[1] And at another time, when the epistle from quarterly meeting was "read and kindly excepted," as the good clerk wrote it, it was quite literally true; for "as to the requeft in the Epiftle from the Laft Quarterly Meeting for Affiftance in Difcharging the Coft ffriends have been at about their meeting houfe in Smithfield we at prefent Defire to be excufed for we are about Repairing our Meeting houfe in S° Kingstown."[2]

The meeting-houses needed continual repairs, and committees are appointed to "ftop ye leak in ye old meeting houfe," or to see to the windows and small repairs, frequently. It was before the days of stoves, and in the long intervals of silent meditation the cold must have been intense.

New England Friends were mindful of the sufferings of Friends in England, and in 1752 the meeting sent £40 14s. by its treasurer, to be taken to the next quarterly meeting to forward to London. The treasurer had a difficult task with his accounts in the variable currency, of which the following entry is an example : —

[1] Vol. I. p. 97.   [2] *Ibid.* p. 35.

It appears by the Records of our Monthly Meeting the 27 of ye Fifth Month, 1747, that there is of the meeting's money in the hands of Peter Davis the sum of £16.16.6 that after the Discount of £13.7 there remains a Balance yet due to the meeting of £3.9.6.¹

Beside the meetings in the meetinghouses, youths' meetings were appointed: one at Westerly lower meeting-house was to be held in the seventh month, "a second day, after the first day." Another was held at William Gifford's, in Charlestown, in the 2d month; a third, in the old meetinghouse, on a fifth day in the seventh month following the second-day meeting at Westerly; and at Westerly upper meeting-house in the second month again.²

So the meeting was fully established with its five houses of worship. First in importance was the old meeting-house on Tower Hill, built on Thomas Hazard's land, which for a nominal consideration he sold to Ebenezer Slocum in 1710, who in his turn transferred it to certain trustees the next day for the same consideration. Then came the two Westerly houses, the meeting-house

¹ Vol. i. p. 111. ² *Ibid.* p. 40.

on James Perry's land in Matunuck and the Richmond meeting-house. What the work of the meeting was, and what manner of men did it, the following pages will endeavor to show.

IV
THE CLERKS OF THE MEETING

IV

THE records of the South Kingstown Friends begin in a small, square hand, with Friends spelled with a double f, and words written as the South County speech pronounced them, and our interest is naturally excited to know something of the man who wrote them. It does not appear from the first record who he was, but a subsequent entry shows him to have been " our ancient friend, Peter Davis." He was a South County man, living near Westerly, who had been prominent in the East Greenwich meeting. Among the first duties that he performed for the new meeting was to " fe to the carrying on " of Westerly lower meeting-house, in which his two sons were appointed to assist him. In 1747, on the 27th of the 2d month, he " Laid before this meeting that there hath been a concern on his Mind for some time to Vifit ffriends in the Weftern parts, and allfo in Europe if the way fhould open for him. And defired a few Lines of ffriends Unity therein." This proposal was considered by the meeting, and two months later action was taken upon it, and the minute is entered by Peter Davis himself: —

1st 4th Mo 1747

Whereas our ffriend Peter Davis is Likely to move from us for fome time this Meeting confidered to Choofe and appoint our ffriend, Stephen Hoxfie to fill his Room in the Service of Clerk to this Meeting. Two certificates for our Antiant Friend, Peter Davis, one for Long Ifland, penfalvenia And ye Jerfes and Verginia &ct Maryland &ct, one for the Ifland of Great Brittian was both writ and Signed in this meeting.

What a journey for a country Friend to set out upon! He calls himself an "Antiant Friend" already in 1747, when he was about to undertake it, though this must have been an honorary title if the record is correct, which places his birth in 1712, which would make him only thirty-five years old. It is possible there is some mistake in this entry, as he lived to a great age, though the record is explicit. He performed his duties to the last, filling twenty-five of the large folio pages with closely written records, and on the 29th of 4th month, 1747, comes his last entry, "This Meeting Ended." One reads it with something of what must have been his own feeling of solemnity at quitting home and kindred. His rule as a clerk was evidently not a very rigid one, for on an occasion "the minits of the Laſt Monthly Meeting not happining to be at hand it was *Remembred.*"

In the spring of 1747, Peter Davis set out on his travels, and certificates as to his preaching were received by the home meeting. The first one is dated from Nine Partners, or, as it was often called, The Oblong, in the Province of New York. This is back of Poughkeepsie, on the Hudson, and for many years was the seat of a famous school under the government of Friends. Peter Davis preached there in May, 1747. The next month found him in the "purchase of Westchester." Woodbridge, in New Jersey, Maryland, Flushing, Long Island, and Philadelphia were visited in turn, and the certificates received, "Which was all Read in this meeting to Good satisfaction."[1] One wonders what his special gift

[1] Vol. i. p. 36.

was, and what aspect of truth he loved to preach. The way opened before him, for after a sojourn in Philadelphia in the autumn of 1747, he sends a certificate from London, dated 22d of 3d month, 1748. No comment is made upon this in the orderly records. There is an interval of six months between the Philadelphia certificate and the one from London. How long a time was he upon the water, one wonders? and what reception did a Rhode Island Friend meet with in London? The records give no indication, but the meeting must have been stirred and stimulated by the fact of its own approved minister carrying his testimony and his gifts so far. In 1751 he was evidently back again, for certificates from The Oblong, Westbury on Long Island, and from the Purchase in the Province of New York, were received. Again, in 1759, it is recorded that "our Ancient Friend, Peter Davis & John Collins hath a concern on their minds to vifit Friends in the Western parts." He was evidently a man of influence in the society, especially where any question of doctrine was involved, and was constantly on committees to deal with offenders against the simplicity of Friends.

He lived to a great age, and was twice married. Content Davis was his first wife, a woman of much influence in the women's meeting. She died in 1781, and he married his second wife, Martha. She "departed this Life the 12th day of the 4th Mo 1809 and was buried the 14th in Friends burying ground in Richmond, aged eighty-eight years." A year before her death the meeting took charge of its aged minister, and a paper exists specifying the food and clothing the aged couple were to have.[1] He lived three years longer, and died in 1812, "aged one hundred years, eleven months and five days," and was buried in the Richmond burying-ground.

A story is told of Peter Davis by the present clerk of the meeting, who in his youth knew an aged man who was his friend. He was vigorous in mind and body, enjoying life to the last. Upon one occasion he was riding along the Matunuck road, erect as usual, and a party of younger friends followed. Thinking him out of hearing, they discussed his great age, saying they would not like to live so long. The old man turned in his saddle and said

[1] Appendix, p. 190.

gently, " Boys, it is sweet to live; I love life." And surely he had had great experience of life. Not only had he more years than any other Friend who is mentioned, but his travels and his preaching had made them full years. He enforced the discipline of the meeting, and the meeting was stringent with him. On the occasion of one of his religious journeys, a committee was appointed to inquire into his conversation and report upon it. They "find things clear concerning Peter Davis. All accept his Setting out on his Jorney before he had a Certificate." Thus even so influential a Friend was kept to the letter of the law.

Stephen Hoxsie, as already noticed, was chosen to succeed Peter Davis when the latter set out on his travels. His first entry, the record of the meeting held the 27th of 5th month, 1747, is a great contrast to Peter Davis's crabbed hand. Peter Davis evidently had modeled his writing after the engrossing hand of the scribe of the day. It was small and square, and lacked the evenness and finish which gave the clerkly hand of the period its character. Stephen Hoxsie begins in a good, flowing hand, and with more modern ideas of spelling, though that retains its "freedom from inforcement" as boldly as the consciences of the founders. South County speech, to this day, speaks of a *convenant* place of meeting, and so the books record it. "Accept" was always an occasion of stumbling, the quarterly meeting epistles being generally *excepted*, while genuine "exception" is often "accepted." But the improvement is great in the fullness and accuracy with which the record was kept. It is a neat-looking record, and for twenty-seven years was written by the same hand. Stephen Hoxsie, and Elizabeth his wife, lived not far from the Richmond meeting-house. They had eleven children, and it was not till a few months after her death, in the autumn of 1773, that he resigned his clerkship. It is his hand that records dealing with debtors, with "disorderly walkers," and notes the proposals of marriage between young Friends. He was often on committees himself to inquire into difficult cases, and was evidently a man of weight and influence in the meeting. He "Departed this life," the record says, "the 24th Day of the 10th Month 1793," within one day of twenty years from the day of his wife's death, "and Was buryed in friends burying Ground at Richmond the 27 of the Same, after a Solid Meeting of friends and others aged 80 years & 26 Days."

This faithful clerk of the meeting was succeeded in 1774 by Peleg Peckham.[1] If Stephen Hoxsie was an improvement on the first clerk, this third clerk was an advance on Stephen Hoxsie. The handwriting has the same general character, but is clearer and firmer, an excellent hand, very legible and distinct. The page has a scholarly air, and the spelling conforms to modern requirements. The use of capitals continues in unexpected places, but the whole record bespeaks a man of better education. The period of the work of this clerk covered the final dealings on the question of slavery, and the whole period of the Revolution. With Peleg Peckham Thomas Hazard was closely associated. In 1775 Thomas Hazard and Peleg Peckham were appointed " to Collect the Several Rules or Minutes of the yearly meeting Tranfmitted to us by Epiftles or other ways & to record them in the Book of Difcipline under their Proper Heads."[2] This was in the first year of Peleg Peckham's service, and all through

[1] Vol. ii. p. 16.   [2] *Ibid.* p. 51.

this period, frequently at the end of a meeting, comes the signature, " Thos Hazard Clerk this Time." I have been in much doubt as to whether Thomas Hazard, who was " College Tom," made these entries himself. Careful comparison with manuscript known to be his would lead to the conclusion that it was. He had an odd way of writing the " s," in the abbreviation of Thomas, high up, close to the beginning of the " H " in Hazard. Either these are his signatures, or his friend Peleg Peckham closely imitated his method. Another circumstance which would seem to indicate that the entries are in Thomas Hazard's hand is the fact that very frequently, in a list of names of a committee, his own name appears last. The first hundred and fifty pages of the second volume of records, covering only seven years, appears to be in the same hand; if by both Peleg Peckham and Thomas Hazard, the resemblance is very remarkable. Nailor Tom Hazard records in 1781, " Cousin Hazard had a fit coming from the mill," and it is in that year that this handwriting stops in the middle of a sentence.

Thomas Hazard was the eldest son of

Robert Hazard and Sarah Borden his wife. His mother belonged to the meeting, but I have found no evidence that his father did. He received a good education, and from the fact of his attending the college at New Haven he derived his nickname of College Tom. He was early exercised on behalf of the slaves, and refused to work his farm with slave labor. He related the occasion of his first turning his thoughts to the subject. In one of the hot summer days between his college terms, his father sent him into the field to oversee the haying. Finding the sun intolerable, he lay down under a tree and took a book from his pocket. But it was too hot to read, and he lay watching the negroes at work. The situation suddenly struck him. If it was too hot even to read in the shade, what right had he to keep men at work in the sun? From that moment his thoughts were turned toward the evils of slavery, and when a little later he heard the stern denunciation of the Connecticut deacon his conscience was fully aroused. "Quakers!" said the deacon, "they are not Chriftian people; they hold their fellow-men in flavery."

Thomas Hazard was a young fellow just

of age, and on the point of being married, when these words were said to him. He gave up his worldly prospects, worked his farm with free labor, and became a zealous advocate of emancipation. His long and useful life has been detailed elsewhere,[1] but in any mention of Narragansett Friends of the eighteenth century he must hold a conspicuous place.

Solomon Hoxsie, a brother of Stephen Hoxsie the clerk, was also a man of mark, often intrusted with business for the meeting. He is called of Richmond, and when he died, in 1781, "was decently interred in his own Burying ground near his houfe."

John Collins was a traveling Friend who belonged to the meeting. He sometimes accompanied Peter Davis on his shorter journeys, and several times the record comes that he "hath it on his mind to vifit ffriends at Oblong." Robarts Knowles was the Friend who traveled with Peter Davis on his extended journey before he sailed for England. A Robert Knowles was under dealing for debt not long after, and one wonders if it was the same Friend,

[1] *Thomas Hazard, son of Robert, called College Tom.* By Caroline Hazard. Houghton, Mifflin & Co.

and if, in his concern for the good of the meeting, he neglected his "outward affairs."

Friends were truly watchful over each other for good. The most prominent men in the meeting were chosen visitors, and overseers of the meeting. The Queries were sent to each meeting from the quarterly meeting, and were not only read in public meetings but in the houses of Friends. They were a list of questions as to the life and conduct of the members. Friends were advised "againſt running into employment they have no knowledge or experience of, but to employ themſelves in that buſineſs they were acquainted with." Their apparel, furniture, table, and way of living was under the observation of the overseers. Nor were the ministers and elders exempt from such supervision, but they were exhorted to have a watchful care for each other.

In 1755 the scope of the overseers was defined when it was

> agreed by this meeting that for the future the viſitors of each meeting Do viſit the families of such who were married among Friends that have not cut themſelves off by Transgreſſion, those who are the chil-

dren of ffriends, and read the Queries to them. And fuch who are willing to be in the obfervation of fuch Queries, and have a Defire to be under the care of friends in order that the monthly meeting may have a Right Sence of the conduct of all Such : and take proper methods to Deal timely with fuch who walk Diforderly.[1]

A little later, in 1761, Thomas Wilbour, Thomas Hazard, and Stephen Hoxsie report still further on the duties of overseers : —

It is our Judgement that every particular contained in the Queries now in ufe in faid Monthly Meetings may with propriety be committed to the charge and care of faid overfeers together with all other Rules of Moral and Religious Conduct that are or fhall be hereafter thought neceffary by faid Monthly Meeting and recommended to their overfight fo far as they do or may relate to the Week Day and Firft Day Meetings and their Members.[2]

Still later the overseers were to take notice of "diforders committed by members,

[1] Vol. i. p. 69.   [2] *Ibid.* p. 122.

viz.: Sleping and all other indecencies," and the omission of members to attend all meetings.

The Queries were reported upon from month to month. In 1754 the visitors report "in fome places Indifferent well, but many places according to our Underftanding too much Indifferency in Regarding the good order which ought to be kept up amongft us for which they Laboured in the ability they Received for Amendment."[1]

A little later, "where there was a Deficiency they generally gave Incouragement of a Regulation." The Queries were also read in meeting, "and friends gave anfwers thereto as proper as they were Capable of at prefent."

The meeting was not afraid to take up grave questions. The question of slavery stirred it deeply; temperance was already a question of the day; education received attention. One question, which was a question in England until very recently, came up in 1771, — the question of marrying a deceased wife's sister.[2] A minute was framed to ask advice upon it in 1772: —

Query to be able to marry a deceafed

[1] Vol. i. p. 63. [2] *Ibid.* p. 245.

wife's fifter or deceafed Hufband's Brother and what is neceffary to be done in fuch cafes?[1]

The system of overseers kept the meeting closely bound together, where "too much indifferency" did not prevail. The most solid men of the meeting were appointed for this service. The Hoxsies, Stephen and Solomon, Peter Davis, and his companion John Collins, and Thomas Hazard, all went from house to house visiting Friends under the care of the meeting. A touch of human nature doubtless crept in on some of these occasions, and the formal reports in the records must sometimes have had their origin in neighborhood gossip. But life was taken seriously, and the daily walk and conversation of Friends was under close observation. In a time of general laxity, and in a new and partly settled country, the orderly rule of Friends made for that righteousness which "exalteth the nation." It may be that the overseers were at times actuated by very human motives, that the quiet country life fostered curiosity. A sense of spiritual pride in those so honored may have crept

[1] Vol. i. p. 267.

in, yet these Friends recognized that their own will was naught; they depended upon the Light of Truth, which they earnestly sought, and, in the beautiful phrase of their clerk, they "labored with the ability they have received."

V
THE WORK OF THE MEETING

V

THE meeting in South Kingstown, though probably the oldest association for worship, was by no means the only one. As early as 1668, the Pettaquamscut purchasers set aside three hundred acres of land, "to be laid out and forever fet apart as an encouragement, the income or improvement thereof wholly for an Orthodox perfon that fhall be obtained to preach God's word to the Inhabitants." The church which was supported from this foundation had teachers at the end of the century, but it was not till 1732 that the Rev. Samuel Niles came, who is called the "firft incumbent of ordination."

These ministerial lands were the cause of a long lawsuit, for the "orthodox person," for whose benefit the deed was made, was held by Dr. McSparran, the missionary of the Church of England, to be no other than himself. Dr. McSparran arrived in 1719, and was active and zealous for many years. His Church of St. Paul's stood in the village of Tower Hill, on the highway leading to the ferry. Dr. Torrey's church, which finally obtained the title to the ministerial lands, stood on the corner of the Queen's high road and the ferry road. The court-house was almost opposite it; and from this centre, in the early part of the eighteenth century, the life of the countryside spread. These two churches are continued in Narragansett. The court-house was moved to Kingstown in 1754. Dr. Torrey's church followed, and has become the First Congregational Church at Kingston. Dr. McSparren's St. Paul's Church was moved to a site a few miles north of the village, and later to Wickford, where the building in which he preached is still preserved. The Church of the Ascension in Wakefield is its South Kingstown descendant. Beside these two established churches at the time of the establishment of the meeting, there were all sorts of minor sects. Beside Quakers and Baptists, Mr. Fayerweather says, "Fanatics, Ranters, Deifts, and Infidels fwarm in that part of the world," and Dr. McSparran bewails the "hetrodox and different opinions in religion that were found in this little corner."

At the same time the good doctor laments this diversity, he speaks of "the power and number of Quakers in this colony." Dr. McSparran does not mention the sect which the Friends had most to fear, if the mention in their records is a true indication, — the New Lights, or New Lites, as Stephen Hoxsie often spelled it. As early as 1748 a Friend was denied his membership because he suffered Friends' meeting "to be difturbed and broken up by the aforeſ^d Wild & Ranting people, which meeting was in his own houſe." Peter Davis and John Collins, the two preachers, who were presumably strong in points of doctrine, were appointed to labor with Henry Mulkins, as "there appears but Little hopes of his Return," and in 1753 he was denied as a "Newlite."

They were also called Separates, or Separators, and the outward sign of a Friend's removing the hat seems to have been taken as a token of falling from grace. A little later two Friends dealt with a man who "has lately joyned with ye People called Separates in their Worſhip ſo far as to Stand up with his Hatt off in the Time of their praying." A second Friend was under the same charge, as he had "attended a meeting of the people called feparators and joined with them in worfhip by taking off his Hatt, etc.," the record says. This reminds one of the early days when the hat played such an important part, and the Boston martyr, William Robinson, exclaimed, "it is for not putting off the hat we are put to death!" One of these Friends confessed his fault as follows:—

I did fometime past Inconfiderately attend a meeting of the people called New Lights, and fo far joined with them in their worfhip as to pull off my hatt which inconfiderate conduct of mine I freely condemn.

In 1767 a young man was under dealing as he "has juftified his union and communion with the Newlights so-called, and Friends being willing that he fhould maturely confider the matter, do conclude to refer it to the next monthly meeting." Two months later his case was again referred, "that his mother may have an opportunity to confer with him." But her arguments did not prevail, and he soon was denied his membership because he "pretended to juftifie himfelf in being Dipp^d in outward water."

As late as 1787 the New Lights gave trouble. A member confessed that he had been to a funeral " and Joined with them in their praying and fo forth, but have confidered my Conduct therein fince and find that I mift it in fo doing," which seems a very modern mode of confession.

The Baptist Church in Wakefield claims descent from these enthusiasts. The shores of Kit's Pond for many years have witnessed converts " dipp^d in outward water ; " and what the good Friends called " Wild and Ranting " was doubtless the fever of exhortation and song into which the neighborhood gatherings wrought themselves. Many of the hymns were a sort of recitation by the leader, with a refrain taken up by the congregation, and punctuated with sighs and groans. A wild religious fervor marked these meetings, wonderful experiences were related, and constant backsliding occurred. To the minds of Friends, they were a people of " dark and erroneous principles." As might be expected, the women's meeting had difficulty with women who were carried away by this enthusiasm. Content Davis, the wife of our ancient friend Peter Davis, was in charge of a case in

1762 where a woman went to the "Separates or New Light" meeting, and with an unconscious arrogance is accused of "joining with them in what they call worfhip." She refused to make satisfaction, and four months after was denied for her "Sade outgoings," as she was "too far joyned into the Religious Sentiments and practices of ye people called New light or Saparates." The following year another woman was "put from under friends care until fhe makes Satisfaction" on the same charge.

The New Light doctrines seem to have been the only religious difficulty Friends had to contend with in Narragansett. It is natural that any revolt from the orderly ways of Friends should go to the furthest extreme possible at the time. Episcopacy and Presbyterianism do not appear to have troubled the meeting. But there were always sins of conduct to contend with, and the meeting kept a watchful eye upon its members. A man was reported as he "had of late tarried at the Tavern unfeafonable and drinked to Excefs his Behaviour and Converfation being diforderly therein," and was duly dealt with. Another man is reported to the South Kingstown Preparative Meeting, as he "had Conducted Diforderly in Selling Spirituous Liquors By Small Quantities without Licenfe."[1] Two Friends were appointed to treat with him.

The young men were dealt with for fighting, which they "openly condemn" as being against "the Peacable principles we Profefs," and also for using "unbecoming and prophain language for which reproachful act I am very forry and do freely condemn," the repentant young man declares. Young Caleb Hazard confesses that he "has of late fo far given way to the paffion of anger as to ftrike and fight with Coon Williams," which he freely condemns. A paper was read at the Richmond meeting-house in August, 1767, which must have caused a good deal of talk before and after the reading. "A man," the writer says,

> come to me in my field and tho I Defired him to Keep off yet made an attempt to beat or abufe me to prevent which I Suddenly and with too much warmth pufhed him from me with the Rake I was leaning on, which act of mine as it did not manifeft to that Christian patience

[1] Vol. i. p. 226.

and Example in Suffering Tryals of every Kind becoming my profeffion I therefore Freely Condemn it and Defire that I may be enabled for the future to Suffer patiently any abufe or whatever elfe I may be Tried with and alfo Defire Friends to Continue their watchful care over me.

Solomon Hoxsie made a complaint of a man " Giving him an occafion of uneafinefs by Charging him with Vfing Deciet with him at feveral times." Thomas Hazard and other Friends were appointed to inquire into the case and make report: " We adjudge that John Knowles condemn his charge of Deceit againft Solomon Hoxfie at fome meeting of friends which the meeting fhall think Confiftent with good order." Another man is charged with using an " Unfavory expreffion, What if you Should Try it out with your guns," which he is advised to condemn.

All cases of dispute were to be adjusted by the meeting, and both parties sometimes gave a binding obligation to abide by the decision rendered. One of the Congdons of Charlestown was complained of by a Friend " for ufing of him hardly in bargaining," and a committee was appointed " to inquire into the Viracity" of the complaint.

Nathan Tucker, who appeared for his father in this case, had to give

his obligation to ſtand and abide the Determination of fuch Friends as Shall or may be chosen and agreed to and fully authorized by faid Joseph and Nathan to Hear Judge and final Determination make of the whole Controversy.... But notwithſtanding the parties are firſt to be Urged to an amicable and equitable fettlement amongſt themfelves and make return of their fuccefs to our next Monthly Meeting.[1]

Friends could sometimes appeal from the judgment of the committee, and a new committee could reconsider the case, as in the following instance: —

The friends appointed to Treat with Dan Bowing Concerning his not complying with the judgement of ffriends in a cafe between him and one of his neighbors Made Report that their Judgment is that friend Bowing ought not to pay anything on that Judgment them friends gave.[2]

[1] Vol. i. p. 230.　　　[2] *Ibid.* p. 68.

In another case there was a difference between two Friends about settling their accounts. The meeting appointed three Friends to assist in settling, and, if they could not do it with the advice of the committee, to "Deliver each of their acco'ts into the hands of the Said Committee and they to fettle them & make Report." They "Completed that affair according to Appointment" 1st 11th month, 1755.

If Friends ventured to appeal to the law instead of to the meeting they were severely dealt with, for St. Paul's maxim was closely followed. A member who had sued his son-in-law, contrary to the good order of Friends, is mentioned. The "Meeting Requefts of him to Defift fuch Diforderly proceedings, and Defires him to attend our next Monthly Meeting to make friends Satisfaction."[1]

In another case, "South Kingftown informed that John Barber has fo far difregarded the Rules of Friends Discipline as to fue a Friend at Common Law." Thomas Hazard and William Robinson were appointed to treat with him, and to inform him "unlefs he makes faid Friend Satis-

[1] Vol. i. p. 92.

faction for the unneceffary coft and trouble he has put him to, and alfo condemn his faid difregard to Friends Difcipline that he will be denied Memberfhip."[1]

Even giving advice as to an appeal to the law was a breach of discipline. A man and his wife are mentioned who " conducted Diforderly in that they advifed and encouraged their fon " to prosecute a friend at common law, and " they are advifed to condemn it."

The meeting was very jealous of the credit of its members. Men were dealt with for not paying their debts, and disowned if they proved dishonorable about it. An example may be taken as a typical case.

In 1766 South Kingstown Preparative Meeting informed the monthly meeting " that it was neceffary a Committee be appointed to infpect the circumftances " of a Friend. John Collins, Thomas Wilbon, and Thomas Hazard were immediately appointed " to go out and treat with faid Robert he being prefent in regard to his circumftances and make Report to this Meeting." This committee reported " that by his Account his Debts and his Eftate are near about

[1] Vol. i. p. 167.

equivalent exclufive of his Houfehold Goods and a few Cooper's Tools the Farm he bought of the Heirs of James Bowdoen and the purchafe money not included." This would seem a large exception, and the committee was instructed " to make further infpection of the Said Robert's circumftances and make Report thereof."

The next month the committee reported, " from his information," the records carefully state, " that he hath bought a tract of land of the Heirs of Bowdoin of Bofton lying in Richmondtown, the confideration three hundred feventy five Dollars to be paid on ye 10 of ye 1 mo 1767. The faid land being vewed by us the Said Confideration in our Eftimation is too much, and further that he hath an Opportunity to enter into the improvement of his brother Samuel's houfe and farm and to have the ufe of one yoke of Oxen therewith at the Rent per annum of 110 yards of Common Shirting flanning and the keep of one Yearling Horfe."

    (Signed) JOHN COLLINS.
       THOMAS WILBORE.
       THOMAS HAZARD.

This year and the year following, 1766-67, were the years in which College Tom made some of his most curious bargains. He bought a horse, a " Dark Coloured Natural pacing Horse " he calls it, in 1766, for fifty-five silver dollars, but the value of the money was to be taken in molasses, indigo, and tea. In the case of this Friend whom College Tom was endeavoring to assist, the bargain for the land was made in dollars also, but the rent to be paid in " Common Shirting flanning," and the keep of a colt, shows how scarce actual money was.

The committee appointed to assist in this case wrote a letter to Boston to endeavor to get Friend Robert released from his purchase, and he reported that he had signed and forwarded the letter, a copy of which was presented to the meeting. As he also proposed " to fell fo much of his perfonal Eftate as would difcharge his contracts, and provide a fuitable place for his family and put himfelf to Labour this meeting advife him to purfue it."[1]

At the 6th month meeting, Friends reported that little had been done toward set-

[1] Vol. i. p. 174.

tling Robert's debts, and at the 9th month meeting the same was true; " therefor as it is not reputable any longer to delay this meeting advifes him to notify his Creditors as foon as conveniently may be and deliver up his Eftate or fo much of it as will fatisfy all his Creditors."

At the next meeting, Friends reported that " faid Robert has concluded to perfue the advice of the Monthly Meeting by notifying his Creditors and deliver up his Eftate to them which is referred to wait for his performance thereof."

It was six months that this Friend had been advised by the meeting, and the case continued much longer. The account of his debts was brought in, which amounted " to fifty eight and three quarters of a dollar, and also Perfonal Eftate Amounting to the Same Sum," which he was desired to " offer up " to satisfy his creditors. The sum seems ridiculously small to modern ears, but the scarcity of money must be remembered. Corn in 1767 was ninety shillings a bushel, and one ewe lamb sold for six pounds in bills. Turned into old tenor, Friend Robert's debts would amount to over £460, which seems a more considerable sum to be advised about. After several months' delay he reported he had only one creditor left, and finally he appeared in meeting and " informed that he had fettled with his one creditor."

But misfortune pursued him, and in 6th month, 1772, he had some very urgent advice. He was first to deliver up the possession of the farm which he had improved for several years to his brother, who had bought it. He is advised : —

2nd that he difpofe of his ftock farming Utenfils etc Sufficient to pay all his Debts. That he accept of the privilege that his Father and Brother offers him (that is the Room in the houfe that he lives in untill next Spring and milk of one Cow this seafon and an acre and a half of land already planted for such a confideration as they have agreed on).

4th [sic] that he put himfelf at labour for the Support of his family what time he hath.

5th that he Endeavour to find Suitable places to put out his Children to trades and learning to fitt them for bufiness, and take friends Advice therein.[1]

[1] Vol. i. p. 262.

Thus closely were the outward affairs of the members under the care of the meeting. Two or three debtors are mentioned who left town without paying their debts, and very plain language is used of them. One man, who was denied for this reason, is informed that "this was a piece of Conduct not only againſt the Rules of the Society but ſcandalous in its Nature and injurious to thoſe to whom he was indebted" in the paper that was publicly read denouncing him. The power of public opinion was thus used for honesty and uprightness.

In another case, Thomas Hazard and Joseph Congdon were appointed to inform a debtor "What friends require of him." This man desired time to settle, "as the weather has been Difficult and he lame," a mode of expression which appeals to one's sympathies. But the meeting was just, and, though they gave time in abundance, finally insisted on satisfaction.

Thomas Hazard was again on a committee which dealt very plainly with another delinquent. It was proposed to Job Irish, "by way of Advice," that he "provide proper place amongſt Friends for his wife and children, deliver up to his Creditors all of his worldly Eſtate to be equitably divided amongſt them, hire himſelf out by the year by Huſbandry or otherwiſe for as much as he can juſtly get, live frugally and make payment ſtill with what he ſhall have to ſpare of his Earnings." This was at the 2d month meeting, 1767, and the vigorous English is doubtless College Tom's. Five months later, " Stephen Hoxſie informed that he had not yet ſent the Writing to Job Iriſh which Friends ordered him to write and ſend." At the next meeting " Stephen Hoxſie is deſired to take care to ſend to Job Iriſh as ſoon as he conveniently can." But at the 10th month meeting he has " yet omitted ſending to Job Iriſh as he was appointed to do." Nine months after the letter was directed to be sent, "Stephen Hoxſie informed that he has ſent forward the letter that he was to write to Job Iriſh, but Friends not having any account whether he has received it or not, therefore that matter concerning him is referred." Early in the next year it was again referred, "as Friends have no account from him, and as it is uncertain whether he received what was wrote to him by the Clerk reſpecting his creditors." Finally, fourteen months after the first action, "This Meeting is informed that Job Irifh has received the writing that the Clerk wrote to him and that he is defirous Friends would yet wait fome longer time with him therefore Friends Condefcends to wait with him until the next Monthly Meeting."

This incident shows clearly the difficulties of communication over the country roads. Matthew Allen, who was a South Kingstown representative when the meeting was set apart at East Greenwich, was once summoned to appear at monthly meeting, but sent excuse, "he being an ancient Man and the Diftance fo far to ride." From Stephen Hoxsie's, near the Richmond meeting-house, to Tower Hill, was indeed a good morning's ride, and Job Irish evidently lived in a remote part of the town. All travel was tedious, even with the good Narragansett pacers, and the consent of the meeting had to be obtained for a journey. On one occasion Robert Knowles "laid before this meeting his intention of going with his wife to Bofton to vifit their Parents and Relatives and defired a few lines of Friends Unity with him." A man and his wife acknowledge "their shortnefs in not advifing with Friends timely" as to their removal, and many certificates are recorded where Friends went on a visit to Long Island or the Oblong.

Indeed, the meeting was kept busy regulating the smaller as well as the larger affairs of life, and keeping closely to the "good order of Friends therein."

VI
THE WOMEN'S MEETING

VI

IT is to the honor of George Fox that he early recognized the value of women's work in the church. There had been Sisters of Charity for hundreds of years before his time, but the cloistered nun had special work, and was shut off from the usual life of women. It was George Fox, who owed so much to Margaret Fell, who first established women's meetings in the church he founded, and made them of equal importance with men's. Among the Friends, trained in habits of independent thought, and early taught individual responsibility, arose women of singular purity and beauty of life, — women of exalted character, and often of great spiritual gifts.

At the establishment of the South Kingstown monthly meeting, the women's meeting, as well as the men's, was set in order and the records regularly kept. These form an interesting comment on the fuller records of the men's meeting, and begin in 1744, a few months later than the men's records. They are preserved in a small quarto volume, which cost fourteen shillings, as the first entry duly records. Anna Perry was the first clerk, and served for fifteen years. Her vagaries of spelling are delightfully individual. The meetings were always called "a Pon," and she was frequently appointed "to Draw an a Piffel to the Quarterly Meeting." It must have been difficult for the women to meet regularly, riding, as they had to, from Richmond or Westerly to Tower Hill, or from Tower Hill to the other meetings. Often, when the meetings were called "a Pon," the entry comes, "So Kingstown now a Pearrence, Westerly now a Pearrence Notwithftanding the Vifitors has Maid Some Progrefs in Vifiting the familys of friends and are in Some Degree Satisfied theirwith," and the "a Piffel" was drawn and signed. In 1758 a new clerk succeeded, as the women were "under a Weighty fence of the Loss it is to the Meeting not having a Clerk Abilitated to Attend the Service." The present clerk informed that she could not, and "the Meeting thinks Proper To be Looking out for one" that may attend. At the next meeting, Mary Hull was appointed, much to the benefit of the spelling. Content Davis, Peter Davis's wife, Abigail Rodman, and Anne Hoxsie were prominent among the women as visitors, and on committees to see to the orderly conduct of marriages. Five shillings were paid for sweeping out one of the meeting-houses; as already noticed, New Lights were dealt with, and the regular and orderly routine of Friends was carefully attended to. In what estimation the women's meeting was held in South Kingstown is well shown by the minute which Thomas Hazard was instructed to draw up in 1771. The Nine Partners' Monthly Meeting had sent "lines" to the South Kingstown meeting, to intimate that it was not according to their practice to receive women Friends unless their certificate was signed by the clerk of the men's meeting: —

Therefore in Condefention to our friends of the monthly meeting at Nine partner's we do hereby direct the Clerk of this meeting to fignifie to s^d monthly meeting that we have neither precedent nor Difcipline amongft us for fuch a practice, neither do we think it Convnant [convenient] So far to Degrade our women's meeting. But to Let them have the Ufe and Exerfife of our Difcipline as occafion may call for it in Conducting the affairs of their meeting not Defiring the Preheminence when Truth admits of none But believing that both male & female are all one in Chrift Jefus.

(Signed) THOMAS HAZARD Clerk this time, 1st day of ye 4 mo. 1771.

The respect with which the women's meeting of South Kingstown was spoken of, though doubtless due to the character of all the women in it, must have been increased by the career of two preaching Friends, Patience Greene, and later Alice Rathbone. As early as 1755, Patience Greene is called a "public friend," and a member of the Society gave Friends "an occafion of uneafiness by his not joining in prayer" with her in a public meeting. The days of open disturbance in meeting were not yet passed; and, after being dealt with, the refractory member appeared in meeting and "faid that he hoped he fhould never give friends the Like occafion for Uneafiness which this meeting takes up with for Satisfaction." The case must have caused a good deal of commotion, for it is several times referred to, and Friends are "cautioned to fhow no Public Marks of Difunion except they have certain Intelligence that fuch a Friend is under Dealing."

Patience Greene had a remarkable career. She was the daughter of David and Mary Greene, called of North Kingstown, both members of the meeting, and, at the time of this public mark of disunity, was only twenty-two years old. An account of her life and services was published shortly after her death. The copy I have studied belonged to Andrew Nichols, also a member of the meeting. She is said to have " Early found in herfelf a propenfity to folly disfipation and vanity." About the age of twenty-one, however, she appeared in "public teftimony," and, until her death forty years later, continued an ardent and valued preacher. After her marriage with Preserved Brayton in 1758, they " were exercifed on account of the Slavery of the Africans," and freed their own slaves. In 1771 she traveled on a religious visit as far south as Georgia, leaving her "infant family feeming to require her nurfing attention," the old Testimony phrases it, and also had the " exercife of parting with a beloved weakly husband." But, smile as we may at the old phrases, it was a noble work she was called to, a work to which she felt herself divinely led. Once they were lost in the woods, where they expected to spend the night, but she says, " I enjoyed more peace of mind upon that reflection than I fhould in fome houfes that were filled with flaves, for that wounds me more than many other evils." She returned home after this long journey, most of it upon horseback, thirteen months from the time she left, to find one child dead and another dying! Later she spent four years in England, from 1783 to 1787, traveling in England, Scotland, and Wales. In the latter country she was much oppressed, as she could not speak the language, and there was no interpreter. As she sat in sorrow thinking this over, and longing to speak to the people, a knock came at the door, and she knew an interpreter had been sent her! And so it proved, for " thus again the Almighty made way for me to my humbling admiration."

Almost all the meetings in England,

small and great, were visited. She went to "our kind friend Lindley Murray's to lodge" at York. "His converfation was reviving to my fpirits," she writes. The prisons were visited. It was still the time when capital punishment was inflicted for robbery, and debtors languished for years in jail. Finally she had a concern of mind to visit the King! The way not opening, however, she sent him an admirable address on the subject of "promoting the freedom of the enflaved Negroes in thy dominions."

It was a woman of this ardent and devoted spirit who preached in the South Kingstown meeting in the freshness of her youth.

Women Friends occasionally came from England, as in 1759, when "our Well esteemed Friend Mary Kirby" brought certificates from London, and her own meeting of Norfolk, England. Her traveling companion was Elizabeth Smith, a member of the Burlington meeting in "West Jerfeys." These certificates were read in the monthly meeting to "good Satisfaction," and the Friends were at liberty to preach in all the meetings.

The women were strict in requiring attendance at meeting. In 1770 a committee was appointed to deal with six Friends for not attending, and for not using plain language. Among the ladies visited College Tom's wife was mentioned. The next meeting, the committee reports " that they find fome making their excufes which they think is fome what reafonable." Elizabeth Hazard and three other Friends report " that they are willing but Difficulties attend their getting out to Meeting." So closely were Friends watched over. The system had its reverse side, as when the young women were dealt with for " keeping company " with one out of meeting. One cannot blame a high-spirited girl for saying, as Hannah Robinson did say, in 1768, when dealt with, " that she has as live Friends would deny her as not." Hezekiah Collins's daughters condemned their being at a marriage " where there was frolicking;" but in spite of that, some Friends were " not fatisfied about what was done about Hezekiah Collins is Daughters," and the acceptance of their apology was reconsidered, with the result of their being denied at the expiration of nine months.

The records of quiet and peaceful doings

among the women are suddenly broken in 1763 by the mention of a woman who was complained of "for offering to Murder her Husband"! Several months afterward she had given no satisfaction, and in 2d mo., 1764, she was denied, as she has of " Late been charged with offering to Murder her Husband, for Which Reproachful Transgreffion fhe Hath been Treated with Several Times." Her first name was Patience: perhaps that was all she had! She lived in Stonington, and one can imagine the excitement of Friends over such an occurrence. In the marriage certificate of this woman she makes her mark only, as her sister does in hers, a rare thing in the case of Friends.

But the great care of the women's meeting was to see that the young women of the Society married in " Younety," as the good clerk Anna Perry spells it in 1745, when a Friend presented a paper which condemned " her out Goings in taking a husband contrary to the minds of friends and is Received into Younety Again." A mother, a few years later, " condemns her forredness in Concenting to her fons marrag And going to the Wedding it being out of the younety of friends." At this day it is difficult to imagine such constant interference with family affairs. But at that time, in the neighboring colonies, the minister was the autocrat of the town. Here in Narragansett, Friends only advised, and the men's records as well as the women's are filled with cases where it was needed.

It was reported to the meeting that William Robinson had given his consent to the marriage of his daughter with a young man not of the Society, "therefore our friends Solomon Hoxfie and Peleg Peckham are appointed to infpect into the ftate of that cafe, and to advife and caution as they find occafion and give us an account thereof at our next Monthly Meeting."[1]

This marriage proceeded, however, and took place in the house, after which there was "vain mirth," and William Robinson was duly dealt with. He acknowledged his offense, and said he had rather "it had been otherways," which the meeting did not accept as satisfaction, and he presented a more humble paper of acknowledgment, which was received. One of the good friends who dealt with William Robinson

[1] Vol. i. p. 202.

on this occasion found a little later that girls are difficult to manage. He did not wait to be complained of, but in 1769 Solomon Hoxfie presented a paper to the meeting in which he gave an account that he "fuffered one of another Society to keep company with and alfo to marry his Brother John Hoxfie's Daughter whom he brought up, which conduct he freely condemned and defired Friends to pafs it by which paper he is defired to read at the end of the Firft Day Meeting where he attends and return it to our next Monthly Meeting."[1]

It makes a curious picture! — a man universally respected and honored, often charged with the grave concerns of the meeting, standing up at the end of worship, and reading his own condemnation for allowing his niece to marry as she wished. If the girl had any affection for her uncle, it must have troubled her sorely to have brought such humiliation upon him.

When marriages were made "in the good order of Friends," the young man and woman appeared in monthly meeting of men and women Friends on a fifth day, and laid

[1] Vol. i. p. 212.

their intentions of marriage before the meeting. They were asked to wait till the next monthly meeting for their consent. In the mean time a committee of men Friends was appointed to inquire into the young man's "converſation and clearneſs as to marriage," and the women's meeting visited the young woman. If these inquiries were satisfactory, when the young people appeared at the next meeting, and "ſignified they were of the ſame mind," the meeting gave consent and appointed two Friends to attend the wedding, to report how it was carried on. One late autumn day, we find, "The weather being Difficult the Young woman Could not be preſent," and the man appeared alone for his answer. The women's record puts it very simply, as when it states that "Sylveſter Robinſon and Alice Perry appeared for their anſwer and had it."

If the lady belonged to a different meeting, the man, "having the Intention of altering his Condition by way of Marriage," desired "a few lines from ffriends of his Clearneſs therein in theſe parts." Newport damsels in this way were often brought to Narragansett.

Consent to marriage was sometimes refused, as with the young man College Tom and Peleg Peckham dealt with. They report that they find "nothing but that he is clear as to marriage, but fome other Branches of his Converfation not fo pure as they Defire." A committee was appointed to treat further with him, but he gave them " No encouragement of Complying with the good order of Truth, therefore this meeting Do not permit him to marry among Friends."[1]

The weddings took place at the meetinghouses at a week-day meeting, when the pair stood, before all their relations and friends, and solemnly plighted each other their troth. " I take this My friend Alice Perry," Sylvester Robinson said, " to be my wife, promifing through divine affiftance to be unto her a faithful and affectionate husband until Death fhall feparate us." The damsel Alice repeated words " of the like import," as the old form phrases it, and the religious part of the ceremony was over. Then the great certificate was signed by the bride and groom, their parents and friends and neighbors, after which came

[1] Vol. i. p. 85.

the festivities, of which the overseers sometimes complained. " Some of the young people were not fo orderly as could be defired," a Friend reports. Some weddings " were pretty orderly carried on," and others " orderly as far as my obfervation," the Friend says. Did the kindly old gentleman turn away from beholding vanity, and, shutting himself in the dining-room with the roasts and the sweets, pay no attention to the " Concourfe of Young people "? For the young people liked to dance then as now, and, if they could not dance at Friends' weddings, there were others in Narragansett where they could. Two Perry brothers are dealt with on this account, and defend themselves in the modern spirit. Our friends Thomas Hazard and Peleg Peckham sign the report, which reads : —

Purfuant to our appointment we have treated with Jonathan Perry and Samuel Perry for their being at an Entertainment fubfequent to a Marriage at which there was vain Recreation. Now here follows the fubftance of Jonathan's fentiment on the affair (viz) that he did no harm nor received any there and that he had rather be in the Meeting. Samuel's sentiments as we understood from what he said amount to this (viz) that he thought there was no harm in keeping the company neither received any at the said Entertainment and that he was willing to send in a paper to the Meeting but neglected to do it although urged thereto.¹

Jonathan Perry afterwards presented a paper condemning his misconduct, but a year or so later he is again reported as attending a wedding and apparently dancing himself, whereupon he is again called to account. Samuel Perry makes explicit acknowledgment : —

Through my too great inattention to the dictates of Truth in my own Mind and attachment to light and vain Company I have been to an Entertainment of late where there was vain Recreation which I too much countenanced and joined with all of which is Contrary to the Good Order of Truth as well as the Discipline of our Society which I look upon to be necessary to restrain Youth from such undue Liberties.

Therefore he condemns his conduct.²

¹ Vol. i. p. 179.   ² *Ibid.* p. 184.

When young Friends actually married out of meeting, they often presented a paper of acknowledgment, and were received again. It must have been rather a bitter thing for a man to present "some lines" even "in some Meafure condemning his mifconduct in marrying out of Unity of Friends," and to have it referred for further consideration.[1] This last paper was still "referred that Friends may have a Sight and Senfe of his Sincerity in condemning his mifconduct." After all, the man was married, and how could he sincerely condemn it if he loved his bride?

One man appeared in meeting and "informed Friends that he had unadvifedly and inconfiderately married out of the Rules of the Society," which he "freely and heartily" condemned.[2]

Another, who had made a marriage contrary to Friends' rules, declared that if they would "pass it by" he would endeavor to be more steady!

A third man presents the following paper, which makes one wonder what kind of woman his wife was: —

    I do hereby acknowledge that I have

[1] Vol. i. p. 212.   [2] *Ibid.* p. 156.

wilfully and knowingly transgreffed the good Order and Rules of the Society in proceeding in Marriage with a woman not of the Society nor according to the Method allowed of amongft Friends for which Transgreffion I am heartily forry and do defire Friends to forgive and pafs by and hope that I fhall by the Lord's affiftance be preferved not only from Transgreffions of fo wilful a kind but alfo from all others.[1]

In 1758 all marriages not among Friends were forbidden by the Society, and Friends adhered to their rules.[2]

This great care for the proper solemnization of marriage is seen to be necessary when we remember that the day of marrying in shifts was not long past. Two cases, among others, are on record in the South Kingstown Records, one in 1719, when the man took the woman in marriage "After fhe had gone Four times a cros the Highway In Only her Shift and hairlace and no other Clothing"![3] The other woman, in 1724, had her "Shift and hair Lace and no

[1] Vol. i. p. 112.
[2] *Ibid.* p. 85.
[3] *S. K. Council Records*, No. 1, 1704-1723.

other clothing on that I fe,"[1] the justice who marries them declares. These were both winter weddings, one in February and one in December, so that humanity, as well as decency and honesty, were outraged. For the object of the curious ceremony was the evasion of debt. If the wife brought her husband nothing, she could not even bring her debts, and he was free from paying them, which he would otherwise have to do.

When such extreme care was manifested by the meeting in regard to marriage, it may well be imagined how severe the dealings of Friends were with immorality. Some young members are on record for "diforderly and fcandalous conduct," and requested to clear themselves of the charges brought against them. Their offenses are described in very plain English, and, no matter what position their fathers had in meeting, they were expelled if the charge was proved true. With Roman fortitude the father in one case signed the document with the other Friends, setting forth his son's misdoing, which was publicly read,

[1] *Town Meeting Records, Births, Marriages*, etc., 1723-1726, p. 69 (from the back of the volume).

denouncing him. In one case, after five years of disfellowship, the young man was received into the Society again, and a certificate given him allowing him to marry. Only one woman in a period of thirty years was dealt with on a similar charge.

We may smile at the quaint phraseology of the records, but it was a good service those women did. Patience Greene, with her gifts of exhortation; Content Davis, visiting the families of Friends; good Anna Perry, with her oddities of spelling, — all did an important work.

In a new country, and in a time of lax morality, the service rendered by the high standard of Friends can hardly be overestimated.

VII
SLAVERY

VII

THE Friends in Narragansett seem to have united, in no common degree, spiritual virtues with temporal prosperity. If they had a David Greene, whose daughter spoke of heavenly things, and left all to preach the gospel, they also had substantial and well-to-do farmers, the Rodmans and Hazards, and others, who, like their neighbors, worked their farms with slaves. South Kingstown was richer in slaves than any other part of Rhode Island, and any effort for the abolition of slavery would be sure to arouse opposition.

It is difficult to determine the exact number of slaves in South Kingstown. The probate records for 1743 mention only nineteen bequeathed by will in that year. The will of George Hazard shows that he possessed fifteen of this number. We have the tradition of the negro election day, when, in imitation of their masters, one of their own number was elected governor; and the laws for the regulation of slaves show that the number was very considerable. As early as 1729 there was a law passed to allow a master to manumit his slave on deposit of £100 security. In 1750 a law was passed forbidding the selling of "strong beer, ale, cider, wine, rum, brandy, or other strong liquor, to any Indian, Mulatto or Negro servant." To guard against evasion, it was specified that no person was to "presume to sell, give, truck, barter or exchange" this liquor with a slave. Slaves were to be within doors at nine o'clock at night, or to be "publickly whipped by the conſtable ten stripes" for each offense. They were not allowed to keep "creaters" in South Kingstown. So it is quite evident that slave-holding formed an integral part of the social order of Friends in Narragansett.

To them came John Woolman in 1748 and 1760, stirring the meeting with his preaching, and his private as well as public testimony against slavery. He and his companions held five meetings in the latter year, when he says he went "through deep exerciſes that were mortifying to the creaturely will. In ſeveral families where we lodged I felt an engagement on my mind to have a conference with them in private concerning their flaves."¹ John Pemberton also came during this period probably, as his letter indicates.² These were saintly men, well tried, and full of faith. These doubtless did not need the caution given by the Discipline of 1775, "to be careful how and what they offer in prayer, avoiding many words and repetitions; and not turning from Supplication into declaration, as though the Lord wanted information." I have elsewhere given the history of the movement against slavery in part,³ but fuller study of the Records has made fresh disclosures. The first recorded testimony against slavery is that of Richard Smith, who presented a paper as " his testimony againft keeping Slaves, and his Intention to free his negro Girl," dated the 28th 11mo 1757. This paper " he hath a mind to lay before the quarterly meeting, all which is referred for further Confideration."⁴ Month after month passed and no action was taken upon it, but the paper remains on record " to fhow the reafon and make it manifeft to mankind why that I difcharge

¹ Woolman's *Journal*, p. 161.   ² *College Tom*, p. 182.
³ *College Tom*, pp. 169–178.   ⁴ *S. K. M. M. R.* vol. i. p. 82.

and fet free my Negro garl named Jane." Then follows an argument against slavery, based upon the Golden Rule, at the conclusion of which comes this personal statement: —

Sometime after I had written this Discharge I had it in Confideration which way was proper to make it Manifeſt & Secure and it appeared to me very proper to lay before Friends at the preparitive meeting, as buifinefs to the Monthly Meeting, to fee if the Monthly Meeting would think proper that it might be put on Record or would forward Untill I might Know what might be done by Friends on this acct. for this thing hath had weight on my mind ever Since this Girl was put into my hands to prove me in this part of Self Denial whether I would be faithfull or not. Now my Friends to tell you plainly Some Years before this my Intent was to have bought Some Negrows flaves for to have done my work to have Saved hireing of help. But when I was about buying them I was forbidden by the fame power that now caufes me to fet this Girl at Liberty for the matter was fet before me in a

Clear manner more Clear than what Mortal Man could have done, and Therefore I believe it is not write for me to Shrink or hide in a thing of fo great Concernment as to give my Confent to do to others Contrary to what we Our Selves would be willing to be done unto Our Selves if we were in Slavery as many of them are at this Day & under Such Mafters and Miftreffes too as would be willing to be called Chrifts true followersand make a Profeffion of fome of his Truths but if we truly Confider God will have no part kept back for he calls for Juftice and mercy and his Soul Loaths the Oppreffing of the Inocent and poor & helplefs and Such as have none to help and will affuredly avenge their caufe in Righteousnefs. Thefe things I have found on my mind to lay before Friends as a matter worth due Confideration and fo lay it before this Meeting as Bufinefs.
(Signed) RICHARD SMITH.

So the principle involved in slavery was very clearly stated as early as 1757.[1]

In 1762 the " Quarterly and Yearly Meet-

[1] Additional Testimony, Appendix, p. 186.

ing Confirmed the Judgement of our Mo^ly Meeting given againſt Samuel Rodman on account of his buying a negro Slave. And it is the mind of friends that there ought to go out a publick Teſtimony and Denial of Samuel Rodman," which was referred to the next monthly meeting. At the next meeting, Stephen Hoxsie was appointed to draw up a "paper of frds Teſtimony of Difowning," as it was the "Sence and Judgement" of the meeting. Notwithstanding this, in 1765 came the Rathbun case, which was before the meeting eight years. Having bought a negro girl, Joshua Rathbun "appeared tender" when dealt with for that disorder, and was brought to confess his error, as follows:—

Westerly: 27th: 12th m° 1765.
To the monthly Meeting of Friends to be held at Richmond next.

Dear Friends. I hereby Acknowledge that I have Acted diforderly in purchasing a Negro Slave, which diforder I was Ignorant of, at the time of the Purchafe but having converfed with Several Friends upon the Subject of Slavery have gained a knowledge that heretofore

I was ignorant of, both as to the Rules of our Society, as well as the nature & inconfiftancy of making Slaves of our Fellow Creatures am therefore free, & do condemn that inconfiderate Act & defire Friends to pafs it by, hoping that I may be preferr[d], from all conduct that may bring Uneafinefs upon Friends for the future, am Willing likewife to take the Advice of Friends both as to the bringing up & difcharging of the afores[d] Negro.[1]

JOSHUA RATHBUN.

This evidently sincere paper was accepted by the meeting, and for some time the matter dropped.

In 1769 occurs this significant entry: —

This Meeting moves the Quarterly Meeting to confider the propriety of the latter part of the 10th Query which is fent up thereto in the Account from this Meeting.[2]

The tenth Query was the query as to slave-holding among members. In this very year the Quarterly Meeting proposed to the Yearly Meeting "fuch an amend-

[1] Vol. i. p. 171.   [2] *Ibid.* p. 212.

ment of the Query of 1760 as fhould not imply that the holding of flaves was allowed."[1] It seems as if this change may have come directly from the South Kingstown meeting. Thomas Hazard had long before freed his slaves, early in the forties, having refused to hold any. Richard Smith in 1757 had borne his testimony against slavery. Samuel Rodman in 1762, and Joshua Rathbun in 1765, had been dealt with, so that the time was coming when a decisive movement could be made.

Such were the conditions when in 1771 Joshua Rathbun made over his negro girl to his son for the consideration of fifty dollars. The money was "made up another way," the record says, the old man evidently trying this to salve his conscience, as he had promised to set the girl at liberty at a suitable age. The son was first dealt with, and denied membership, because he

> Encouraged the Deteftible practice of enflaving Mankind by his takeing a bill of sale of a negro girl of his Father and afterward Sold her fo that She was carried out of the Country notwithftanding

[1] *Publications of the R. I. Historical Society, Slavery in R. I. 1755-1776*, W. D. Johnston, p. 148.

his promife to his sd father to Sett her at Liberty at a Suitable age.[1]

The father was desired to try to recover the girl, and even advised to "Commince and profecute" his son "for the Recovery of Damages upon a promis" made by the son, which he failed to do.

The meeting held at Joshua Rathbun's house was ordered discontinued in 1771, as he "did not ftand Clear in his Teftimony for the Caufe of Truth as he ought to have done" against Slavery. But he replied two years later, during which time he apparently continued the meetings, that "he fhould be glad to take friends' Advice but hath peace in holding faid Meetings apprehending it as he faid as his duty."[2] His wife was dealt with by the Women's Meeting, and acknowledged her offense in sitting in a meeting out of unity, though it was in her own house, and finally the old man was denied his membership.

Ten Friends are mentioned in 1771 who were under dealing about their slaves. Old Dr. Rodman, who lived by the dam on the Saugatucket where Peace Dale now is, " appeared in this meeting, and Saith that

[1] *S. K. M. M. R.* vol. i. p. 260. [2] *Ibid.* p. 276.

he fhall not comply with the Rules of the Society Refpecting his Slaves to Liberate them."[1] Some members " appears of a difpofition to comply with friends rules in liberating their flaves," but five Friends, among them two women, one of whom was College Tom's mother, Sarah Hazard, widow, " did fhew the Contrary Difpofition." Three were denied membership. Sarah Hazard must have been converted by her son, for only one woman proved obdurate, and was " noticed " to the Women's Meeting.[2]

In the women's records, the first mention of " the bufinefs concerning flaves " occurs at the 12th month Women's Meeting, 1771. It was continued and reported upon for a year, when the paper of denial was drawn up. The disowning of this woman is dated 23d day of the tenth month, 1772, and is a noble testimony from the Women's Meeting. She is denied her membership, as —

of late it doth appear that She hath Refufed to comply with that part of our Difcipline which is againft the enflaving Mankind a Practice very repugnant to Truth and Equity an invation of the

[1] *S. K. M. M. R.* vol. i. p. 245.   [2] *Ibid.* p. 245.

Natural Rights of Mankind fubjecting them to a ftate of Bondage and oppreffion wolly Inconfiftent with the Spirit of the Gofple now having dealt with her According to the order of the Gofple in much Labour and forbearence that the oppreffed might go Free. But fhe Conueth to Difobey the Truth and reluctant to our advice on its behalf We have Denied her Memberfhip in our Society until She return To the Truth and make Satiffaction for her Tranfgreffion which is our Sincear Defire This teftimony Given forth in behalf of the Truth and againft Tyranny & Oppreffion from our Monthly Meeting of Women Friends held at Richmond the 23 day of Tenth month 1772.

Signed by ten women.

At the 4th monthly meeting, 1771, a committee was appointed to treat with all who " poffes flaves." They were kept busy for two years, and in 1773 report that "they dont find there is any held As Slaves by Frds."[1]

Notwithstanding this encouraging entry in the records, the committee to visit slave-

[1] *S. K. M. M. R.* vol. ii. p. 1.

keepers was still continued, and found a little more to do. A list of emancipated slaves gives the names of five liberated in 1773,[1] and eight more who were freed at intervals till 1786, which was two years after the Emancipation Act had been passed by the Rhode Island legislature. But the meeting had clearly declared its principles, and stood boldly for liberty.

It is interesting to follow the course of the men denied. Among them, Joshua Rathbun claims our sympathy most of all; and the following touching letter, written two years after his denial, is in conformity with all we can glean of his character:—

ye 12th Day of the 5 month 1775.

Deare friends have had a mind Ever fence my Denial toock Place uppon me to be under the Care of friends yea with great Defire at times: But Sea no way for it as my mind Stood: I deare Do no other way But to be Honeft to what Sence I had: it was a great Crofs to me to be Denied by friends it was all moft two much for me to beare: How Ever I was Boorn up under it all: and have not

[1] Appendix, p. 190.

as yet fainted: bleffed be God for his Preferving Power that he might in his own time give me Sight and Sence: and at Lenth: the Lord has Shewed me by the Inftance of Eli: that I Should not only have advifed: my Son: but Should have Conftrained him to have Done Juftis to the black garl: and I Sea now I Should have taken up with the advife of friends: in Proficuting my Son, if he would not have Done Juftis with out: and I am Sorey that I Could not at that time have taken up with the advife of the Laft Committey to me Sent By the monthly meating Namely: John Collins Solomon Hoxesey thomas Wilber & Joseph Congdon advifing me to Defift and not hold no more meattings for friends had no Eunity with it. I Say I am Sorrey Seeing it was a Crofs to the Difcepline of friends and as to the manner of my holding of meattings out of Eunity I freely Condem: and as to the matter Leave me to Stand or fall to my own mafter: and I Defire that friends may Pafs it by and take me under there Chriftion Ceare: I Never Saw as I now Sea till ye 7th of this Inftant: from one that Defiers to travel no fafter then the Light Difcovers and to Comply with Every manyfeft of it: Who allfo Defires to be admitted a member of your Sofiatry.

JOSHUA RATHBUN

It is a comfort to find the following report, which was duly recorded, and to know that the old man was doubtless reinstated: —

According to appointment We have had an oppeturnity With Joshua Rathbun Refpecting his Requeft to be Reftored again to Memberfhip With friends and he appears to be in a Good Degree Sincere in his Requeft Which We think Well of Granting him all Which We Submit to the M° Meeting Next to be held at Richmond.

PETER HOXSIE
THOMAS WILBUR
WILLIAM J. KNOWLES
JOSEPH CONGDON

He died, aged 77 years, the 14th of 7th month, 1801, " of a very diftreffing Diforder in his Stomach, which he endured with much Fortitude and Refignation and which terminated his Life the Evening of the fame day."[1]

As late as 1800, Joshua Rathbun the son desired to be restored, and was favorably reported to the meeting, as he " appears to be in a Good Degree Sincere in Condemning his Mis-Conduct." He also "faid he Was Willing to do all he Could to Relieve the Negro Girl from Slavery that he was Denyed for Selling." And in 1807 comes a letter from Benjamin Rodman, who was denied in 1772.[2] He was Dr. Thomas Rodman's son, and writes to the meeting: —

South Kingstown the 26th of 2d Mo 1807.

In confequence of Friends dealling (as I then thought, too hardly with my father) many years ago, refpecting his keeping of Slaves, which I was so unguarded as to refent, and to refufe to Set at liberty thofe in my poffeffion, which have fince all been liberated by me,

[1] *Births, Marriages, and Deaths*, p. 146.
[2] *Ibid.* p. 265.

which conduct of mine (in refufing to free them at that time) I am forry for and defire friends to pafs it by and again admit me as a member of Society.

BENJ. RODMAN

To the Mo. Meeting of friends
next to be Holden at
Richmond.

These papers really show the power of the meeting. To Joshua Rathbun it came as a bitter trial to be denied; to the other men, in their way, either as a discredit or a misfortune, which years after was remembered, and repaired if possible. It was the power of public opinion about them — the consensus of opinion of the best and most honorable men they knew — that they valued, as well as the doctrine of the church they loved. So, in a formative period of American history, these little self-governing bodies of men, scattered in remote rural districts, bound together by ties of love and belief, and a common purpose of daily life, — these little meetings had vast influence in training men to public affairs, in shaping the true democratic policy toward which the country was tending. The meeting might seem isolated; but while such men as John Woolman and John Pemberton came to it, while Mary Kirby from England crossed the water to visit it, it was not out of communication with the great world. Out to that world it sent its own ministers, Peter Davis, Thomas Robinson, and Patience Greene, who, under her married name of Patience Brayton, could not have forgotten the meeting of her youth. The very fact of the beautifully printed London Epistles coming yearly was an education, and the books which the meeting subscribed for made many a good Friend's library. It was the existence of many such well-governed and self-sustaining bodies as the South Kingstown monthly meeting which made possible our Revolution, paradoxical as this may seem, since any resort to arms was so severely discountenanced. Here, in small, a truly representative government was in operation.

VIII
THE REVOLUTION

VIII

THE middle of the eighteenth century certainly marked the height of the greatest power and usefulness of the South Kingstown meeting. The long agitation over the question of slavery, which began as early as 1742, at the time of Thomas Hazard's (son of Robert) marriage; which was discussed in John Woolman's powerful sermons, and personal pleadings with masters and mistresses in 1748; to which Patience Brayton and Richard Smith bore testimony in the fifties, — was finally settled in meeting in 1773. This was a formative period. A question affecting the lives of so many persons, masters as well as servants, naturally stimulated thought; and, though the meeting was in a little corner of the world, it was not left without leaders from abroad, as well as those developed within its own borders.

Two Friends in especial throw light upon this period, — the diary of Jeffrey Watson, beginning in 1640 and ending 1783; and that of "Nailor Tom" Hazard, from 1778 to 1840, the two covering a period of one hundred years of observation by men of unusual capacity and intelligence. Both these men were Quakers by birth and training. Jeffrey Watson was the son of John Watson, Esq., the first child born in Narragansett after the Indian War,[1] his obituary notice declares, that is, in 1676. " He was bleft with more than a common fhare of good fenfe, and was early employed in many important affairs." At his death, at the age of ninety-seven years, he left one hundred and thirty-eight descendants, a great part of whom followed him to the grave. "He was a Loving Husband, a Tender father, a juft Magiftrate, a good neighbor, a mild Mafter, and an Honeft Man." Our ancient friend, Peter Davis, preached at his funeral, also Stephen Richmond and Robert Knowles. His son, Jeffrey Watson, inherited many of his father's good qualities, and seems to have had a special relish for preaching. In 1743 he records having heard at Friends' meeting " the ableft man that I had ever heard in

[1] I am indebted to Mrs. C. E. Robinson for a copy of this valuable diary.

my life." He mentions all the special meetings of Friends, as in 1755: —

I was at the Quaker Meeting and there was two Old England and one Fillydelphia man fpoke exceedingly able.

Again in the same year: —

I was at the Quaker Meeting to hear Saml Fothergill. There was a boundance of people the minifter Exceedingly Able and a great fcolar Difcourced in a very High Stile.

Watson also went to the Baptist meeting. Once it was held in the woods, on a rainy day, but Gardner Thurston preached a very able sermon from Joshua, 24th chapter and 16th verse. Again, at the Baptist meeting, Samuel Albro is recorded as exceedingly able, preaching from the text, "Prepare to meet thy God o Ifreal."

Thomas Hazard is mentioned as a preacher; in 1791 the text of his funeral sermon for John Watson, senior, is given: "The Grace of God has appeared to all Mankind."

All the prominent Friends' funerals are spoken of. They departed this life with "Much Lamentation" he often adds. Of the other preachers, Hoxsie is often mentioned, the good clerk of the meeting. Whitman preached from the ever comforting text, "Bleſſed are the dead who die in the Lord." Patience Greene preached often in 1756 and 1757, and Stephen Richmond later. So the meeting was well supplied with its own ministers.

Some hint of the state of the currency is given in June, 1757, when, at Tower Hill, "they was a letting bank money." After a few days' consideration, on the 9th of June Watson went to Tower Hill "to Take of the Bank money." This was one of the issues of paper money which Rhode Island had made at intervals from 1710. The premium was enormous; the issue of 1757 is quoted at £5 15s. for one Spanish milled dollar, while the next year the value of the silver dollar rose to £6 in old tenor bills.[1]

In 1761 comes an interesting record:—

Jan. 19. This Day the Prince of Wales was proclaimed King of England by the name of George the Third by the Grace of God King over Great Britain France and Ireland, Defender of the Faith &c.

There were still some years when the

[1] *R. I. Colonial Records*, vol. vi. p. 361.

orderly proceedings of the meeting were quietly carried on, but there were signs of the coming storm. The debased currency was in itself a source of danger. In many instances barter was resorted to again, and contracts had to provide in what sort of money they should be paid, since every year saw increased inflation. Corn, which in 1751 sold at twenty-five shillings a bushel, gradually rose till in the early sixties it reached its maximum of one hundred shillings. Careful men of business kept their accounts in old tenor and lawful money, with endless trouble and confusion. No wonder Jeffrey Watson often records trying to settle accounts, "but could not do it," and his joy when he has finally agreed with a certain creditor, and makes the record, " fettled accounts for ever and ever amen "! Then came the stirring days of the Revolution. In Narragansett the echoes of the shot that rung around the world were also heard. It is interesting to find some of the earliest advice to Friends was in regard " to receiving and paffing the late paper Currency that is made and paffed in thefe Colonies Iffued Expreffly for the purpofe of Carrying on War it is recommended to friends Serious Confideration and Obfervation."¹ This was given from Newport in 1st month, 1776. Friends in the summer of that same year were advised to "enter deeply into themfelves and not implicitely follow the fentiments of others, but fee that their proceedings therein are in the liberty of the Truth."² So powerful were the Quakers in the Colony that the General Assembly passed an act in June of the same year entitled " An Act for the relief of perfons of tender confciences, and for preventing their being burthened with millitary duty."³

The meeting therefore drew up a minute instructing Friends how to act under the circumstances : —

This meeting is informed that through late Laws Friends are fubjected to fome penalties on certain Requefitions which they may be releafed and excufed from by Producing a certificate to the chief Officers from our Clerk Setting forth that they are members of the Religious Society called Quakers, therefore the clerk

[1] *S. K. M. M. R.* vol. ii. p. 55.
[2] *R. I. Meeting Records*, 1776.
[3] *R. I. C. R.* vol. vii. p. 568.

is directed to make and fign Certificates to our members applying for the fame when no diforder or irregularty doth appear and every fuch applying member is earnestly defired to Examine and fee that nothing be done out of the truth that our Teftimony may be preferved pure and no reproach brought upon friends.[1]

A meeting for Sufferings was early arranged, and members who had suffered on account of military service were instructed to send " the account and prices there of in Value of s^d Sufferings to the clerk of this meeting and for the Clerk to Tranfmit An acc^t to the meeting for Sufferings."[2]

But the war began to press home. Thomas B. Hazard, called " Nailor Tom," in his diary begins to note the movement of vessels with an anxious eye. From the ridge of Tower Hill the bay lay in plain sight, and Newport was always an important point. He writes : —

Jan. 30, 1779. The Regulars landed and took two boats out of the river. 4 sail went upland from Newport. Some snow. One ship went into Newport.

[1] *S. K. M. M. R.* vol. ii. p. 51.
[2] *Ibid.*

The next month "Davis privateer went eastward;" March 20th, "a sloop sailed out of Newport about sunset." May 8, "Regulars landed in Point Judith." Nailor Tom was a man of great conversational power, if tradition is to be trusted. He could picture a scene most vividly, and his conversation was enlivened by flashes of wit and humor; so that for him this last brief entry doubtless called up the whole scene, and he felt again all the commotion of the countryside. But, fortunately for us, Jeffrey Watson gives a fuller account of this proceeding. The entry in his diary is May 9, 1779:—

John Gardner Jun was Taken at Point Judah with his 9 workmen by the Land Pirates who Joyned the Miniftered party to burn plunder and Deftroy the Inhabitants of North America and took ye faid Gardner's eftate from him nine oxen Twenty fix cows with their calves and about forty five fheep with their lambs and caryed to Newport the 8 Day of May 1779 and kept him prifoner until Oct 15 1779. Job Watfon had about feven hundred fheep with their lambs caryed of at the same time and some cattle. June 25. Land pirates Landed again of Point Judah and caryed away from John Gardner between two and three hundred wait of cheefe two lambs and fome of his wifes wearing clofe and fome other fmall things and from Job Watfon two negro men and four white men that was at work for him. Gorton was feen this day in a Bean field near by where they landed.

Nailor Tom makes two or three entries that same month. June 3d, "Craddock was taken in his fifh boat by the Privateersmen." The 6th, " Regulars landed and took Samuel Congdon." The 8th, " The Regulars burnt two houfes laft night." The 12th there was an "alarm in the night." So the countryside had its share of disturbance and tumult.

Jeffrey Watson makes an interesting entry in 1781 : —

March 6 General Wafhington Rode by our Houfe with about Twenty Soldiers for a guard about ten o'clock.

He was born in Virginia in the county of Weftmoreland the eleventh day of February 1732. Had a Col's commiffion at nineteen years of age was taken Prisoner by the French and Indians and given Liberty on a Parol was exchanged when Gen. Braddock was Defeated near Dequefne in the year 1755.

The meeting records have occasional references to dealings with members who acted "in the Quality of a Soldier." As early as the 27th of 5th month, 1776, a young man is reported who had enlisted and

> gone into the Millitary service which conduct being Inconfiftant with the Principles of Truth which we profefs and contrary to the Teftimony which we as a people have always bourn, Wee therefore Deny him remaining any Longer a Member of our Society.[1]

Other dealings with delinquents follow. One man who paid a war tax was labored with, as this was contrary to the " General teftimony againft contributing toward carrying on War." Another member is denied for " hireing such eftates as are faid to be confifcated."[2] But the general conduct of affairs was not apparently interrupted. On the very same page on which this political offense is recorded, equal space, if not more, is given to the consideration of a man who married again within four months of his

[1] *S. K. M. M. R.* vol. ii. p. 63. [2] *Ibid.* p. 103.

THE REVOLUTION 169

wife's death, and, further, "that the said John has lately joined with ye people called Seperators in their worſhip ſo far as to Stand up with his Hatt off in time of their praying."

Another good Friend was denied because he bought some books at a vendue, taken from a vessel which was a prize of war, although he pleaded that he thought "his motive being to Reſtore the moſt Valuable Book purchaſed to the Right Owner was a Mitigation of his Tranſgreſſion."[1]

The 31st of 8th month, 1778, the monthly meeting was informed that the old meeting-house "has been lately occupied as a Hoſpital for the ſick lately landed out of the French fleet and greatly Damaged and likewiſe the pale and board fences wholly deſtroyed."[2] A committee was therefore appointed " to apply to the Barrack Master, (and others whoſe right and buſineſs it may be) requeſting the reparation " of the house and fences.

Young men were drafted, and others hired to go as substitutes; but in general the "labour for their recovery" proved ineffectual. In 1780 comes an entry that

[1] *S. K. M. M. R.* vol. ii. p. 132.   [2] *Ibid.* p. 109.

throws more light. A matter came up against a man who had resided in Newport for several years, and "the Communications with the main being Obſtructed Untill late laſt Fall by its being a Britiſh Gariſon and ſince the Evacuation the Severity of the Seaſon and other Impediments hath hitherto prevented the Committee appointed from Treating with him."[1]

During this time the agreement from the meeting for Sufferings in Providence, of which Thomas Hazard, son of Robert, was a member, to raise funds for a school by subscription, was received, and the matter duly reported upon. The temperance question was also coming into prominence, and Friends bore their testimony against persons who "drinked to exceſs," and those who "ſold Spiritous Liquor by the ſmall quantity without a Licenſe."[2]

Attending a horse-race also came within the limits of disorderly conduct, and the lines of Friends were drawn even more strictly in this time of trial and disorganization. In 1775 a committee was appointed "to reviſit such perſons as Choſe to be conſidered as members of our Society," and

[1] *S. K. M. M. R.* vol. ii. p. 149. [2] *Ibid.* p. 170.

they were to be informed "that it is the Defire of this meeting that they duly attend all the meetings both of worfhip and Discipline, and alfso Maintain Our Chriftian Teftimony in every Branch thereof."[1]

Attending Jemima Wilkinson's meetings was a cause of stumbling, for which a paper of contrition had to be presented.[2]

South Kingstown had a "concern," in 1781, "to take under further confideration the Neceffity of Bearing a Teftimony againft War & Fighting and alfo our Testimony for Plainnefs of Speech and Apparrel."[3]

So the careful regulation of the daily life of Friends continued. It was an important influence in a formative period of our history. The "good order of friends" had to be strictly observed. Each little meeting had its definite relation to the larger meetings. The overseers were appointed by the monthly meeting to take charge not only of "Sleping and all other indecencies" in the meeting itself, but of conduct; and any deviation from the strict rule of Friends was reported to the preparative meeting,

[1] *S. K. M. M. R.* vol. ii. p. 42.   [2] *Ibid.* p. 171.
[3] *Ibid.* p. 172.

which made its returns to the monthly meeting. This meeting could refer difficult cases to the quarterly meeting, or advice could come from the quarterly meeting. The quarterly meeting in turn could appeal to the yearly meeting, the final source of authority. This government fostered independence of thought and speech, for it rested upon the consent of the governed; members were only " fuch as chofe to be confidered friends." The papers of contrition all ask to be "received again into the loving care of friends." It was a voluntary submission to what each man considered best and right.

But the great service Friends rendered was a spiritual service. We, who have to trace the history of a single meeting in records which are of necessity accounts of delinquencies, may be apt to forget the great principle for which they stood, — "the light of Truth within me," as the old testimonies phrase it. It was the doctrine of the indwelling Spirit which gave those men their power. In an age of formalism, when true religion languished and bigotry still reigned, George Fox proclaimed this doctrine. No wonder he was misunderstood. No wonder that even such a man as Roger Williams, with his bold teaching of freedom of different consciences from inforcement, shrank from this still bolder assertion of the divine light and truth dwelling in each soul. To him this seemed a blasphemous assumption. And indeed, in the freedom in which the early Friends rejoiced, they did carry their conduct to extremes. In protesting against outward forms, they sometimes offended the decencies of life. But in the eighteenth century these eccentricities had in large measure disappeared. Thomas Hazard, the Hoxsies, Collins, and the other prominent Friends of the meeting were grandsons of the men who heard George Fox preach in Justice Bull's house on Tower Hill. The meeting was settled and in order. They had the tradition of piety and right living behind them; they knew the truth which had made them free. The churches around them were still in bondage to the minister. Episcopacy was struggling for a foothold in the New World, and here was an organized representative government fully equipped for work, and with the vital spark of life.

It had fought the battle of emancipation. For years it quietly worked with its members, until long before the act of abolition in Rhode Island, passed in 1784, the South Kingstown meeting was clear in its testimony against the "deteſtable practife of enflaving Mankind." It stood for temperance in all things, — in its rebuke of intoxication, in its sobriety of speech and behavior, in discountenancing unseemly amusements. If " dancing and vain mirth " at weddings were counted among these, we must remember the license of the times, and how seldom these recreations were kept within proper bounds. It stood for education. Books were subscribed for. Fox's " Journal," and " Barclay's Appology now printing at Philadelphia," was sent for. Sewall's " History of Friends," " Piety promoted," the "reprint of the Holy Bible," are all mentioned; and when the school was established, in 1781, South Kingstown took its share.

It stood for equal rights of men and women. Many a minute closes, " The women's Meeting being in unity there in." This equality was based on a broad and firm foundation, the men's meeting " not Defiring the Preheminence where Truth admits of none But believing that both Male & female are all one in Chrift Jefus."[1] So the women had training in independent thought and action. To them, questions of conduct were often referred: they had, as women always must have, charge of the aged and the poor. They themselves treated with women who held slaves, and were thoroughly competent to take care of their own meeting. Elizabeth Kirby and Patience Greene were preachers held in honor by the whole meeting, who traveled, the first from England and the latter to England, speaking the message which was delivered to them, "according to the measure of their ability." These meetings had an important share in preparing the country for self-government. The man second only to Washington himself belonged to the Greenwich meeting, to which the Narragansett meetings also belonged until 1743. Who can doubt that the training in administration, as well as in high principle and true courage, stood Nathaniel Greene in good stead in his eventful career? The habit of plain speaking and righteous dealing gives tremendous power; and when to

[1] *S. K. M. M. R.*, vol. i. p. 235.

that is added a true recognition of Divine guidance, a constant turning to that Inner light of Truth the possession of which is the birthright of every child of God, we should expect heroes from such a nurture. It was a high ideal that those just men set before themselves, and an ideal which led to practical results in ways they could not approve. The same freedom they taught their sons, the same liberty they claimed for themselves, led to the throwing off of British rule, and, through the "war and carnal fightings" they so deeply deplored, to that larger liberty in which a new experiment in civilization could begin.

APPENDIX

A
Quaker's Sea-Journal
Being a True
RELATION
of a Voyage to
NEW ENGLAND
Performed by Robert Fowler of the Town of
Burlington in Yorkſhire in the
Year 1 6 5 8

London Printed for Francis Coſſenet at
the Anchor & Mariner in
Tower-Street   Anno 1659

A true Relation of the Voyage undertaken by me ROBERT FOWLER, *with my ſmall Veſſel called the* WOODHOUSE *but performed by the Lord like as he did* NOAH'S *Ark, wherein he ſhut up a few righteous perſons, and landed them as ſafe, even as at the Hill Ararat.*

The true Diſcourſe taken as followeth:

THIS *Veſſel was appointed for this ſervice from the beginning, as I have often had it manifeſted unto me, that it was ſaid within me ſeveral times,* Thou hath her not for nothing, *and alſo New England preſented before me; alſo when ſhe was finiſhed and fraughted, and made to Sea, contrary to my will, was brought to* London, *when ſpeaking touching this matter to* Gerrard Roberts, *and others, who confirmed the matter in behalf of the Lord, that it muſt be ſo; yet entring into reaſoning and letting in temptations and hardſhips, and the loſs of my life, wife and children, with the enjoyments of all earthly things, it brought me as low as the grave, and laid me as one dead, as to the things of God, but by his Inſtrument G. F. was I refreſhed and raiſed up again, which before that it was much contrary to my ſelf, that I could as willingly have died, as have gone, but by the ſtrength of God I was made willing to do his will; yea, the cuſtoms and faſhions of the Cuſtom-Houſe could not ſtop me: ſtill was I aſſaulted with the Enemy, who preſſed from me my ſervants, ſo that for this* *long Voyage we had but two men and three boys, befides my felf. Upon the firft day of the fourth Moneth received I the Lords fervants aboard, who came with a mighty hand and an outftreched arm with them, fo that with courage we fet Sayl and came into the Downs the fecond day, where our dearly beloved W. D. with* Mich. Tomfon *came aboard, and in them we were much refrefhed, and after recommending us to the grace of God, we lanched forth: Again reafon entered upon me, and thoughts rofe in me to have gone to the Admiral, and have made my complaint for the want of my fervants and a Convoy, from which thing I was withholden by that hand which was my helper: Shortly after the South winde blew a little hard, fo that it caufed us to put in at* Portsmouth, *where I was furnifhed with choice of men, according to one of the Captains words to me,* That I might have enough for money, *but he faid my Veffel was fo fmall, he would not go the Voyage for her. Certain days we lay there, wherein the Minifters of Chrift were not idle, but went forth and gathered fticks, and kindled a fire, and left it burning; alfo feveral friends came aboard and vifited us, in which we were refrefhed: Again we lanched from thence about the Eleventh day, and was put back again into* South Yarmouth, *where we went afhore, and in fome meafure did the like; alfo we met with three pretty large fhips, which were for the* New found Land, *who did accompany us about 50 leagues, but might have done 300, if they had not feared the Men of War, but for escaping them they took to the Northwards, and left us without hope of help to the outward, which before our parting it was shewed to H. N. early in the morning, that they were nigh unto us that sought our lives, and called unto me, and told me, but said he, thus saith the Lord, you shall be carryed away as in a Mist, and presently we espied a great Ship making up towards us, and the three great Ships were much afraid and tacked about with what speed they could for it; in the very interim the Lord God fulfilled his promise, and struck our enemies in the face with a contrary wind, wonderfully to our refreshment: then upon our parting from these three Ships, we were brought to ask counsel at the Lord, and the word was from him,* Cut through and steer your streightest course, and minde nothing but me, *unto which thing he much provoked us, and caused us to meet together every day, and he himself met with us, and manifested himself largely unto us, so that by storms we were not prevented above three times in all our Voyage; The Sea was my figure, for if any thing got up within, the Sea without rose up against me, and then the Floods clapt their hands, of which in time I took notice, and told H. N. Again in a vision in the night I saw some Anchors swimming above the water, and something also of a Ship which crost our way, which in our meeting I saw fulfilled, for I my self with others, had lost ours, so that for a little season the vessel ran loose in a manner; which afterwards by the wisdom of God was recovered into a better condition than before: Alſo upon the twenty-fifth day of the ſame Moneth in the morning, we ſaw another great Veſſel making up towards us, which did appear far off to have been a Frigot, and made her ſign for us to come to them, which unto me was a great croſs, we being to windward of them; and it was ſaid,* Go ſpeak him, the croſs is ſure, did I ever fail thee therein? *and unto others there appeared no danger in it, ſo that we did, and it proved a Tradesman of* London, *by whom we writ back: Alſo it is very remarkable, when we had been five weeks at Sea in a dark ſeaſon, wherein the powers of darkneſs appeared in the greateſt ſtrength againſt us, having ſayled but about 300 leagues H. N. falling into communion with God, told me that he had received a comfortable Anſwer, and alſo that about ſuch a day we ſhould land in* America *which was even ſo fulfilled; Alſo thus it was all the Voyage with the faithful, which were carried far above ſtorms and tempeſts, that when the Ship went either to the right or left hand, their lines joyned all as one, and did direct our way, ſo that we have ſeen and ſaid, we ſee the Lord lead our Veſſel, even as it were a man leading a horſe by the head, we regarding neither latitude nor longitude, but kept to our Line, which was, and is our Leader, Guide and Rule, but they that did, failed. Upon the laſt day of the fifth Moneth we made land, it was a part of the* Long Island *far contrary to the expectation of the Pylot; Furthermore our drawing had been all the Voyage to keep to the Southwards, until the evening before we made land, and then the word was,* There is a Lion in the way, *unto which Lion we gave obedience, and said, Let them steer Northwards until the day following, and soon after the middle of the day, there was drawings to meet together before our usual time, and it was said, That we may look abroad in the evening, and as we sate waiting upon the Lord, they discovered the land, and our mouthes was opened in Prayer and Thanksgiving; as way was made, we made towards it, and espying a Creek, our advice was to enter there, but the will of man resisted, but in that estate we had learned to be content, and told him both sides was safe, but going that way would be more trouble to him; also he saw, after he had laid by all the night, the thing fulfilled.*

Now to lay before you in short, the largeness of the Wisdom, Will and Power of God, Thus this Creek led us in between the Dutch Plantations and Long Island, *where the moving of some friends whereunto, which otherwise had been very difficult for them to have gotten too: Also the Lord God that moved them, brought them to a place appointed, and us into our way, according to the word which came to C. H.* You are in the road to Road Island. *In that Creek came a Shallop to meet us, taking us to be strangers, making our way with our Boat, and they spoke English unto us, and informed us, and also guided us along: The power of the Lord fell much upon us, and an unrestable word came unto us,* That the Seed in *America* shall be as the sand of the sea.

It was publifhed in the ears of the Brethren, which caufed tears to break forth with fulnefs of joy, fo that prefently for thefe places they prepared themfelves, which were Robert Hoggen, Richard Dowdney, Sarah Gibbins, Mary Witherhead, *and* Dorothy Waugh, *which the next day we put fafely afhore: Into the Dutch Plantation called* New Amsterdam, *we came and it being the firft day of the week, feveral came aboard on us, and we began our work: I was caufed to go to the Governor, and* Robert Hoggen *with me; he was moderate both in words and actions.* Robert *and I had feveral days before feen in a vifion the Veffel in great danger; the day following this was fulfilled, there being a paffage between two Lands, which is called by the name of* Hell-gate, *we happened very conveniently of a Pylot, and into that place we came, and into it were forced, and over it was carried, which I never heard of any before that was; and the Scripture is fulfilled in our eyes, in the Figure,* Hells gates *cannot prevail againft you: rocks many on both fides, fo that I believe one yards length, would have endangered lofs of both Veffel and Goods; Alfo there were a fcull of fifhes purfued our Veffel, and followed her ftrongly, and along clofe by our Rudder; and in our meeting it was fhewed me, Thefe fifhes is to thee a Figure, Thus doth the Prayers of the Churches proceed to the Lord for thee and the reft: furely in our Meeting did the thing run through me as oyl, and did me much rejoice.*

FINIS

Copied in the British Museum, July 5, 1897, by C. H.

RICHARD SMITH'S TESTIMONY AGAINST SLAVERY.

I Richard Smith of Groton in the County of New London and Colony of Connecticut upon Confideration and Knowing it Required of me I have written this in Order to Show the reafon and make it manifeft to mankind why that I Discharge & Sett free my Negro Girl named Jane at Eighteen Years of Age Daughter of Sarah which is now in Slavery with her other Children Among the kein of Stephen Gardner of Norwich Deceafed their Girl Jane was Given to my Wife Abigail by her Father Stephen Gardner by will in Order to be a Slave all her Days According to the Common Cuftom of Slavery. But She falling into my hand by my Wife and the Lord by his free Goodnefs having Given me a clear Sight of the Cruelty of making a Slave of one that was by Nature as Free as my Own Children and no ways by any Evil She had Committed brought herfelf into Bondage and Slavery and therefore can no ways be Gilty of Slavery, and to argue becaufe her Mother was made a Slave being by force and Violence brought Out of her Own Land againft her mind and will and Deprived of What She had there & made a Slave of her Should be a Sufficient Reafon that her pofterity Should be Opreft in bondage with Slavery. I fee no Juftice for it nor Mercy in fo Doing but Violent Opprefsing the Inocent without Caufe For this thing of Servants it hath pleafed God to fett before us in a

Clear manner the cafe of Servants and Especially the Unreafonablenefs of thefe mafters and miftreffes who profefs to be the followers of Chrift how they will buy & fell and be pertakers in making Marchandize in Great Babylon of the Slaves that is the bodys of men and women and of thefe Strangers as Indians & Negrows that are taken Out of there Own Country or taken in War one among a nother and Sent out which when brought here in Sed of being Relieved are Sold into Slavery all there Days and there pofterity after them they being never fo Innofent in Ronging of any and thefe masters and miftreffes that buy them or Other ways by their parents have them, all this while profefs them-felves to be the followers of Chrift or Chriftians and yet how they will plead the Reafonablenefs of Keeping them in Slavery and their pofterity after them. But when they have pleaded all they can and ufed the beft Arguments they have, it is only to have there work done with eafe & they to be great and to be Lord Over there fellow Creatures, Becaufe they have power & Authority to Opprefs the helplefs by a Cuftomary Law of the Nations to keep them in Bondage under Slavery, Quite Renouncing and rejecting and Hating to Obey the Law & command of there great Lord and Mafter Chrift as they call him who charge them faying Therefore all things whatfoever ye would that man fhould do to you do ye even fo to them for this is the Law and the prophets faid Our Great

Lord Matt. 7 & 12 Now if it ſhould be aſked of any of theſe Maſters or Miſtreſſes if they in like Manner with there Childeren ſhould be carried away unto any Strange People in the world and be Sold into Slavery whether they would be willing to Serve a ſtrange Nation in Slavery & their Children after them and be Deprived of what they Injoyed in there Own Country (for this is the Caſe) I Suppoſe there Answer would [be] no nor any of Our Children upon any acct. No not if they were in a Chriſtian Land as they call this Well then how can any of them plead the Reaſonableness of Keeping of any of them in Slavery with there poſterity and not to ſet them free in a Reaſonable Time as they themſelves with their Children would be willing to be done by According to Chriſts words above mentioned for by Nature all Nations are free One from the Other and the apoſtle Saith God is no Reſpecter of perſons, the Apoſtle Likewiſe Saith that God hath made of One Blood all Nations of men to Dwell on all the face of the Earth Acts 17 & 26 So that by Nature & Blood we are no better in Gods Sight than they and it is plain that Chriſt taught a Doctrine that was to releive the Oppreſſed and to Unbind heavy Burdens and let the Innoſent priſoners go free, and hath Commanded us to love Our Enemys, and to entertain Strangers, & not to Oppreſs them in Bondage with Slavery and Said, he came not to Deſtroy Mens Lives but to ſave them Luke 9 & 56 So that the way that brings them into Slavery is forbidden

by Chrift for by war Violence & Stealth and tradeing in them is the way by which they are firft Ordered to go into Slavery, and they that buy them or otherways have them and keep them in Slavery as they do there Beafts for to do there Labour & not to releive them and fet them free, are pertakers of the Same evil, Therefore I Leave this as a faithfull Teftimony in the fear of the liveing God againft all such wicked proceedings, and upon true Confideration of what is written I hereby Declare that now at this Time that my Negrow Girl Jane hath arrived to Eighteen Years of Age that fhe Shall now go out Free from Bondage and Slavery as free as if fhe had been free born and that my Heirs, Executors or Adminiftrators fhall have no power Over her to make a Slave of Her or her pofterity no more than if She had been free born, for I freely give her her freedom now at the arrival of the aforefd age which is now fullfilled in this prefent Year 1757 as witnefs my hand
 (Signed) RICHARD SMITH.

LIST OF PERSONS OWNING SLAVES, NAMES OF SLAVES AND DATE WHEN SET FREE

Name of slave	Owned by	Date of emancipation
Jane	Richard Smith	1757
Pegg	Stephen Richmond	27th 12th mo 1773
Phillis and her two children Casper and Judith	John Knowles	1st 11th mo 1773
Richard	Jeremiah Browning	27th 9th mo 1773
Israel	William Robinson	15th 1st mo 1780
Dick	John Congdon	29th 12th mo 1783
Luce, Jack, Fan	William Congdon	29th 3d mo 1784
Cuff, otherwise Cuff Knowles	Barshebe Knowles, Robert Knowles, Joseph Knowles, John Congdon, Charles Congdon, Hannah Knowles	24th 7th mo 1783
Job	William Peckham	4th 8th mo 1786
Rose	William Peckham	24th 8th mo 1786

PETER DAVIS' OLD AGE

We the Committee appointed to provide for the Support of Peter Davis and wife have met on ſd Buſineſs and propoſe the following agreement made with Peter Hoxſie for one years ſupport of ſd Peter Davis and wife that He will keep Martha Davis for the conſideration of her Anuity or income free & clear from any expence to friends, and that he will keep and support Peter Davis includeing victualling, clotheing, Doctrineing, lodgeing &c for the ſd term of one year, for the conſideration of fifty dollars, twenty Seven of which is due to the ſd Peter Davis from Wm Sweet Peckham, which he agrees to Collect of him, which will leave twenty three Dollars for the Monthly meeting to pay, — Or in that Proportion if the f^d Peter should deceafe before the expiration of that time. And the f^d Peter Hoxfie agrees that they fhall be as well clothed at the years end as they are when he receives them — his year is to commence the 8th day of the 7th Mo. 1808.

All which we fubmit to the Mo. Meeting.

PETER HOXSIE
JOHN CONGDON
JEREMIAH BROWNING, JR.
JOSEPH COLLINS, JR.

Hopkinton the 10th of 7th Mo.
A. D. 1808.

INDEX

INDEX

ADVICE to debtors, 109.
Albro, Samuel, 161.
Allen, Matthew, 112.
Aquidneck, 5.
Arnold, Benedict, 7.
Atherton, Humphrey, 51; death of, 52.
Austin, Anne, 10.

Barber, John, 104.
Books subscribed for, 174.
Bounds of meeting, 65.
Braddock, General, 168.
Bradstreet, Simon, 5-51.
Brand, William, 15.
Brayton, Preserved, 121.
Briggs, John, 54.
British garrison, 170.
Bull, Jireh, 48.
Burnyeate, John, 49.

Cartwright, John, 49.
Clark, Mary, 13.
Collins, Hezekiah, 124.
Collins, John, 87.
Congdon, Joseph, 59.
Congdon, Samuel, 167.
Commissioners of the United Colonies, 3.
Copeland, John, 13.
Corn, price of, 163.
Creditors, 108.

Dancing, 130.
Davis, Content, 99.
Davis, Nicholas, 25.
Davis, Peter, 63; his travels, 78; his old age, 81.
Deceased wife's sister, 90.
Debts and debtors, 105.
Diman, Professor J. L., 5.
Dyer, Mary, 24; sentenced, 26; letter to the court, 27; on the gallows, 29; reprieved, 30; executed, 35.

Easton, Nicholas, 6.
Endicott, John, 9, 26.
Epistles, London, 156.

Fayerweather, Rev. Mr., 96.
Fisher, Mary, 10; in Turkey, 14.
Fothergill, Samuel, 161.
Fowler, Robert, 10.
Fox, George, 12; meetings in Newport, 46; in Narragansett, 48; established women's meeting, 117.
Friends denied, 169.
Friends' judgment in controversies, 103.
Friends' meeting accounts, 73.
Friends' spiritual service, 172.
Friends' sufferings in England, 72.

George III., proclaimed, 162.
Gibbons, Sarah, 15.
Gorton, Samuel, 6.
Greene, David, 139.
Greene, Nathaniel, 175.
Greene, Patience, 120; her travels, 122–23.
Greene, Peter, 54.

Hazard, Elizabeth, 124.
Hazard, Robert, 86.
Hazard, Sarah, 148.
Hazard, "Nailor Tom," 160; diary, 165.
Hazard, Thomas, 59; serves as clerk, 85; frees his slaves, 86; preaching, 161.
Holder, Christopher, 13.
Horse-racing, 170.
Hoxsie, John, 127.
Hoxsie, Solomon, 87; makes complaint, 102; marriage of niece, 127.
Hoxsie, Stephen, 82.
Hutchinson, Mrs. Anne, 5.

Inflated currency, 67.
Irish, Job, 110–112.

Kirby, Mary, 123.
King's Province, 50.
Knowles, John, 102.
Knowles, Robert, 87; visits Boston, 112.

Laws against Quakers, 18.
Little Rest, 62.
Liquor license, 101.
Longfellow, 17.

Marriages, 128.
Marriage in a shift, 133.

Marrying out of unity, 132.
McSparran, Dr., 95.
Meeting-house in Greenwich, 53.
Ministerial lands, 95.
Mulkins, Henry, 97.
Murray, Lindley, 123.

New Lights, 97–100.
Nichols, Andrew, 121.
Niles, Rev. Samuel, 95.
Norton, John, 15.

Old meeting-house, 62.
Overseers, 91.

Paper money for war purposes, 163.
Peace Dale, 147.
Peckham, Peleg, 84.
Pemberton, John, 141.
Perry, Alice, 128.
Perry, Anna, 118, 125.
Perry, James, gives land for meeting-house, 68.
Perry, Jonathan, 130.
Perry, Samuel, 130.

Quakers, acts of law against, 18.
Quakers, travelling, 23.
Queries, 88–90.
Query, the tenth, 146.

Ranters, 4.
Rathbun, Joshua, 144; sells his slave, 146; denied, 147; restored to membership, 150; death, 153.
Rathbun, Joshua, Jr., 153.
Rawson, Edward, 22.
Records of meeting, 77.

Regulars at Point Judith, 166.
Rhode Island, the "back door," 22.
Richmond meeting-house, 69.
Robinson, Mrs. C. E., 160.
Robinson, Hannah, 124.
Robinson, Rowland, 54.
Robinson, Sylvester, 129.
Robinson, William, 24, 126.
Rodman, Benjamin, 153.
Rodman, Samuel, denial of, 144.
Rodman, Thomas, 54.

Separators, 97.
Sewall, Samuel, 51; entry in diary, 62.
Sewel, historian, 16.
Slave legislation, 140.
Slaves in South Kingstown, 139.
Slaves in the women's meeting, 148.
Slocum, Ebenezer, 62.
Smith, Elizabeth, 123.
Smith, Richard, frees slave, 141.

Temperance, 170.
Testimony against war, 168.
Torrey, Dr., 96.

Tower Hill, 49; letting money at, 162.
Tucker, Nathan, 103.
Thurston, Gardner, 161.

Upsal, Nicholas, 11; banished, 21.
Usquepaug, 70.

Watson, Jeffrey, 159; accounts, 163.
Watson, Job, 166.
Watson, John, 160.
Washington, George, 167.
Waugh, Dorothy, 15.
Westerly meeting-house, 66.
Whittier, "A Spiritual Manifestation," 43.
Widders, Robert, 45.
Wilbour, Thomas, 89.
Wilkinson, Jemima, 171.
Williams, Roger, 8; charter procured by, 41; goes to Newport, 47.
Winthrop, Governor, 6.
Woman's meeting records, 118.
Woodhouse, voyage of, 12.
Woolman, John, 140.

Youths' meetings, 73.

www.ingramcontent.com/pod-product-compliance
Lightning Source LLC
Chambersburg PA
CBHW020921230426
43666CB00008B/1525